19 Gifts of the Spirit

Which do you have? Are you using them?

Leslie B. Flynn

While this book is designed for the reader's personal use and profit, it is also intended for group study. A leader's guide is available from your local bookstore or from the publisher.

VICTOR BOOKS®
A Division of Scripture Press Publications Inc.

All quotations in this book are used by permission of the copyright holders, which are noted in connection with each particular quotation. To these copyright holders, we express our thanks. In addition, we wish to credit the following:

Creative Bible Teaching, Lawrence O. Richards, © 1970, Moody Press, Moody Bible Institute of Chicago. *One People,* John R. W. Stott, © 1968 by John R. W. Stott; used by permission of Inter-Varsity Press, Downers Grove, Ill. *Managing Our Work,* John W. Alexander; revised edition; © 1972 by Inter-Varsity Christian Fellowship; used by permission of Inter-Varsity Press, Downers Grove, Ill. *Body Life,* Ray C. Stedman; © 1972 by Ray C. Stedman; Gospel Light Publications, Regal Books Division, Glendale, Calif.

22 23 24 25 26 27 28 29 30   Printing/Year 94 93 92

Library of Congress Catalog Card No. 73-91027
ISBN 0-88207-701-5
© 1974, SP Publications, Inc.
Printed in the United States of America

VICTOR BOOKS
A division of SP Publications, Inc.
          Wheaton, Ill. 60187

DEDICATION

To the memory of my parents,
James A. Flynn and Agnes G. Flynn,
who passed away, both in their 89th year
within 6 weeks of each other, in 1972,
whose gifts were more serving than speaking,
who exercised them with great grace.

THE AUTHOR / Leslie B. Flynn serves as a senior pastor of Grace Conservative Baptist Church of Nanuet, New York. He graduated in 1940 from Moody Bible Institute (pastor's course), and later earned a B.A. from Wheaton College, a B.D. from Eastern Baptist Theological Seminary, and an M.A. (philosophy) from the University of Pennsylvania. In 1963 the author received a D.D. from Conservative Baptist Theological Seminary. He has long been active as an author and for 15 years was an instructor in journalism at Nyack Missionary College. His other books under the Victor label are:

The Other Twelve
The Twelve

Contents

PREFACE

A talented organist before the days of motor-driven or electric organs gave a magnificent concert in which the big pipes sent forth glorious, thunderous tones. After people finished congratulating him, the little boy who had worked away with all his might at the bellows behind the curtain remarked, "*We* did pretty well, don't you think?"

The organist disdainfully replied, "And what did you do?" He gave the boy no credit at all.

A month later, during another concert, the organist came to a stormy passage that required all the wind of which the bellows were capable. Suddenly the organ began to fade away. The organist signalled for more wind. Just then the little lad pulled aside the curtain and bargained, "Then shall it be 'we'?"

When the organist nodded vigorously in the affirmative, the lad went to work with a will.

Today great emphasis is being laid on the "we" in the need for everyone's gift—not just the pastor's—to play its part so that the church's melody of truth and love may sound forth with harmony, beauty, and volume. Hence, the subject of charismata, the gifts of the Spirit, finds deep interest in the ecclesiastical world.

In this book both enumeration and classification of gifts are given non-dogmatically. The author realizes that scholars have differences of opinion, finding more or fewer gifts and arranging them in various categories. However, the listing and grouping in this volume appeal to the author as having merit.

Recent surveys show that many people are profoundly dissatisfied with their jobs. How can we face every morning with keen anticipation and fresh outlook? Were we to awake to each new dawning with the assurance that the Lord had given us spiritual gifts through which He planned to make us a blessing to others that day, would not this make rising eager and exciting?

If high schoolers, housewives, working men, and business women were to head out each day, not to school or housework or place of business, but to the ministry for which the Holy Spirit had equipped them, would not this help to make the day's employment purposeful, zestful, and abundant?

To face each day with this conviction, we first need to know the nature of the gifts the Spirit has given the church. Then we need to discover, develop, and deploy our spiritual abilities.

The author is convinced that almost every Christian has more gifts than he realizes. Also, even though a person may have only a few of the gifts, he is nevertheless responsible to be practicing obedience in the areas of most of the gifts. Thus, a discussion of all the gifts can serve as a reminder of a host of Christian duties, even when gifts in those areas are absent.

The purpose of the gifts is to build up other believers. In an ancient fable the stomach was accused of doing nothing and consuming everything. So hands and feet and teeth decided to go on strike and send nothing to the stomach. Result was—they began to waste away. The stomach proved to be important as it shared with other organs to make them healthy. As each believer employs his gifts, the church is edified.

Part I
Charismata: the Gifts of the Spirit

1
Me a
Gifted Child?

The superintendent of a Sunday School approached a soft-spoken chemist about teaching a class. The chemist, a Christian for two years, responded, "I have no gift. When God gave out spiritual gifts, He missed me!"

When the same superintendent contacted another member, a lawyer who had been a believer for five years, his answer was, "I'm sure God must have given me some spiritual gift, but I really don't know what it is or how to discover it!"

Down the street in another church, a long-time believer was running in circles doing 14 different jobs, few of them effectively. In his heart he knew he didn't possess enough gifts to serve in so many capacities.

In still another church, a new convert, a well-educated man, was prematurely assigned to teach the college class. As the class began to dwindle, it became evident that he didn't have the gift of teaching. To salvage the situation the superintendent dismissed him, perhaps too abruptly. His feelings hurt, the ex-teacher rarely attends church today. The superintendent wonders, "If we had helped him discover his gift in a more cautious and prayerful manner, might he be serving the Lord in our church today, though in some other capacity?"

The subject of spiritual gifts, important in the life of the Early Church but too often neglected through the centuries, has recently risen into prominence in modern church thinking.

Apostolic believers learned early in their Christian experience

9

the truth about gifts. When the young church at Jerusalem faced the complaint of discrimination in the administration of daily welfare, the apostles urged believers to seek out godly and *gifted* men to handle the problem. So the congregation chose men with the gift of wisdom. The result was an increase in the ministry of the Word and in the number of disciples (Acts 6:1-7).

Paul wrote about gifts in his letters to the Romans, Corinthians, and Ephesians. In fact, these letters give us three major lists of gifts.

Paul taught about gifts from the very beginning of every new church. He wished each assembly to develop spiritually in normal and undelayed fashion. New churches with all new believers had no members adequately mature to qualify as elders or deacons. But thrown on the power of the Holy Spirit to put into practice Paul's teaching on the discernment and discovery of spiritual gifts, some members grew sufficiently to be chosen as elders on Paul's return visit, not long later (Acts 14:21-23). Through the exercise of gifts, saints had been edified.

Sadly, too often through the years, the church has failed to encourage its members to utilize their gifts. Pastor has done much, but people little. A bit of doggerel composed by an anonymous clergyman's family goes like this:

> *"The Rector is late,*
> *He's forgotten the date,*
> *So what can the faithful do now,*
> *Poor things?*
> *They'll sit in a pew*
> *With nothing to do*
> *And sing a selection of hymns,*
> *Poor things!"*
>
> (*One People,* John R. W. Stott,
> Inter-Varsity Press)

A pastor was reviewing the church membership rolls with his official board. Scribbled after several names were the initials, FBPO. After a while one of the board members asked, "Pastor, explain the meaning of those letters."

Replied the pastor, "They mean—For Burial Purposes Only. You see—these are our inactive members!"

God would have taken us to heaven immediately at conversion

had He no purpose for us here. Among other purposes, "we are saved to serve." To equip for service, God gives one or more spiritual gifts to every child of His. He does not want "deadwood" in His church.

Pastors unwittingly discourage the development of spiritual gifts if they play the "I've-got-to-do-everything" superstar role. All the while, spiritual gifts lie dormant in laymen who should be sharing in the ministry by teaching, leading, counseling, evangelizing, and in many other ways.

Today, the renewed interest in spiritual gifts is manifesting itself in many ways. Seminary classes and pastors' seminars are being devoted to this topic. Some Christian leaders who never gave serious study to the subject are being confronted with it. A pastor who was interviewing a prospective Christian education director had the tables suddenly turned on him when the Christian Ed candidate, taking advantage of a lull in the conversation, asked, "Pastor, what do you consider to be your spiritual gifts?"

The pastor, though over 25 years in the ministry, confessed, "I never really gave it much thought before this moment!"

Dr. Earl D. Radmacher, president of Western Conservative Baptist Seminary, in an article, "The Jack-of-All Trades Syndrome," writes, "Every pastor ought to have a goal of helping each member to identify his gift, and then to find the place where his gift fits into the total work of the church. It is a rare pastor who has preached a series of messages covering each of the spiritual gifts. I ask pastors I meet, 'Why don't you take 15 weeks and preach on one gift of the Spirit each week and then ask for decisions from your people?' Ask them, 'What are your gifts? How are you using them?' And really dig in deep because, as I understand it, shaping up the saints in large part means enabling them to find out what their gifts are and where they can use them" (*Moody Monthly,* March 1971).

On the other hand, some congregations have rediscovered the role of the layman. They afford opportunities for use of gifts. Laymen lead Sunday morning services, call on sick and shut-in members, visit the unchurched, and lead in plans for new ministries.

In one parish, composed of half a dozen rural congregations and served by only one full-time ordained minister plus a student intern, all six congregations have Sunday morning service every single week. A corps of 19 lay preachers lead church worship. On any given Sunday, the pastor and his assistant will preach in two of the churches, and the other four pulpits will be filled by four of these lay preachers.

Practice of the biblical doctrine of gifts untaps reservoirs of godly manpower, thaws out frozen assets, roots out unemployment among saints, reflects the universal priesthood of believers, and edifies the church.

As the church comes alive today in the area of gifts, many questions are being asked, such as the following:

What is a gift?

How are gifts related to talents?

How many gifts are there? What are they?

Are all the gifts listed somewhere in the New Testament?

How are gifts related to the fruit of the Spirit?

Do gifts differ from offices?

If a person has teaching ability, will he automatically have the gift of teaching?

How may a Christian discover and develop his gift?

Does the average Christian have just one gift or several?

Are all the gifts for today, or did some cease at the end of the apostolic age?

What place has the gift of tongues in today's church? The gift of healing? Miracles?

If a person doesn't have the gift of evangelism, is he excused from trying to win people to Christ?

Should a church have a gift-conscious committee to guide church leaders in finding what gifts the Holy Spirit has given members of that congregation, then aligning these people with some ministry in the church for exercise of their gift?

This book will attempt to answer these and other related questions.

No Ungifted Believers

Every child of God has a gift or gifts. Our gifts are assigned us when we are born by the Holy Spirit into the family of God. At the moment of a believer's baptism into the body of Christ at regeneration, he is given a gift which he should exercise for the health of the whole body. Though gifts may lie dormant for months or years, they are given at our spiritual birthday. The word for gift was used by the Greeks to refer to a birthday gift. The presence of gifts from the moment of conversion explains how in the Early Church some could qualify for elder or deacon not long after the founding of a new fellowship.

Paul emphasized the universality of gifts. "Unto *every one of us* is given grace according to the measure of the gift of Christ" (Eph. 4:7). "The manifestation of the Spirit is *given to every man to profit withal*" (1 Cor. 12:7).

Without exception, every new believer receives a gift or gifts. Those fresh from heathenism—new believers in Brazil, Zaire, India, and Taiwan—have been given spiritual gifts. Also unschooled converts are the recipients of gifts, for gifts have no relation to education.

Even those with wicked backgrounds are allocated gifts immediately on repentance. Though the Apostle Paul had been a violent persecutor of the church, even to sharing in the death of saints, the Spirit gave him gifts the moment he was saved. The Corinthians possessed gifts in abundance, despite only a few months removal from flagrant sinning (1 Cor. 6:9-11).

So, you are a gifted child of God. Since you are also given an outlet for your gift, you are a minister too. Three days after confronting Jesus on the Damascus Road, Paul was told by Ananias that his ministry was to bear the name of Jesus before Gentiles and kings (Acts 9:15; 22:15, 21; 26:16-18). For every gift He bestows, the Spirit has planned a sphere of service.

Thus, no child of God should have an inferiority complex. Rather, awareness that he is a gifted child with an area of ministry should meet every child of God's psychological need to feel wanted and to possess a sense of worth. No false humility should make him moan, "I'm a nobody," and lead him to bury his gifts and hear the ultimate verdict: "slothful servant."

To sum up—though not every believer is exercising his gift, nor even knows what it is, nevertheless every child of God has received one or more gifts to be used for the upbuilding of the church, and for which he will one day render account.

Gifts Are Varied

A well-known conductor was holding a rehearsal one night with a vast array of musicians and a hundred-voice choir. The mighty chorus rang out with peal of organ, blare of horns, and clashing of cymbals. Far back in the orchestra the piccolo player thought, "In all this din, it doesn't matter what I do." Suddenly the conductor stopped the music, flinging up his hands. All became quiet. Someone, he knew, had failed to play his instrument. The shrill note of the piccolo had been missed.

Just as many notes are needed to make harmony, and many colors to make a painting, so many gifts are essential for the functioning of the body of Christ. Paul put it, "For the body is not one member, but many" (1 Cor. 12:14).

We are not born equal. Though we share in the same Holy Spirit, who enables all believers to confess Jesus as Lord (1 Cor. 12:3), and who has baptized all believers into the body of Christ (v. 13), we are given different spiritual gifts for service. More than once Paul uses the analogy of the human body with its many members —eyes, ears, hands, feet—to illustrate the varied gifts in the church of Christ. "Ye are the body of Christ, and members in particular" (v. 27).

How many different gifts are there? Some list as few as 9; others in the range of 15 to 22; and still others estimate many more. An attempt to catalogue the gifts will be made in chapter 3.

How many gifts are assigned to each believer? At least one, likely more than one, perhaps several. Could not this be inferred from Christ's parable of the talents in which one man was given one, and another two, and another five? Though one fellow had only one, the other two had a total of seven talents between them.

We can also observe multiple gifts in operation in individuals described in the New Testament. For example, Philip had the gifts of wisdom, showing mercy, evangelism, and perhaps others unrecorded in the sacred record.

Two or more gifts may often operate simultaneously, blending together. Just as a candle on a three-branch candelabra may shine separately and distinctly while the other two remain unlit or two or three may shine jointly, so a person may have just one gift in exercise, or at another time gifts may glow co-mingled.

Not only are we appointed diverse gifts, but we are allocated differing ministries. Since each believer has a different combination of gifts and ministries, it's likely each of us is in some way unlike any other believer in arrangement of spiritual abilities and outlets to serve. We may not be created equal, but we are unique. There will never be another you.

Why do we get differing gifts? And why do we get the particular gifts we do? The sovereign Holy Spirit simply assigns to every man individually as He wills (1 Cor. 12:11; Eph. 4:7). "God set the members every one of them in the body, as it hath pleased Him" (1 Cor. 12:18). Clearly, distribution of gifts is by divine dealing.

Therefore, no one should boast of his gifts. Paul asks, "Who maketh thee to differ from another? and what hast thou that thou didst not receive? now if thou didst receive it, why dost thou glory, as if thou hadst not received it?" (1 Cor. 4:7) Because our gifts come through the gracious sovereignty of the Spirit, and not through any merit of ours, they should occasion no bragging on our part.

Neither should we follow, nor idolize, nor become the devotees of any human leader out of admiration for his gifts. Paul warns against this error in 1 Corinthians 3, pointing out that those who exercise the gifts must not be allowed to eclipse Him who gave them (see vv. 3-7, 21-23). Leaders are only fellow-servants, gifted by the Spirit for a particular ministry.

This means we should never envy anyone else's gifts—not Billy Graham's evangelism ability nor John Stott's teaching expertise. Rather, we should be content with God's choice of gifts for us. Discontent is really criticism of the way the Spirit runs His church.

Margaret loved to entertain but found teaching impossible. When she accepted God's sovereign wisdom in bestowing on her the gift of hospitality, she entertained frequently, and was a real blessing to her guests. Barbara, on the other hand, enjoyed teaching, but found it hard to entertain. When she accepted her gift of teaching, guilt feelings over failure to entertain as much as Margaret dissolved. Barbara entered zestfully into teaching her Bible classes, also blessing many. Margaret and Barbara thanked God for each other's gifts instead of envying them.

Your Gift Is Not For Your Sake

Complying with the law for compulsory military service in Argentina, a fellow showed up at the induction center objecting, "What good would I be? I have no arms!" They put him in the army anyway.

At basic training camp, his commanding officer said, "See that fellow up there on the hill pumping water? Go tell him when the pail is full. He's blind!"

Gifts are given us to build up one another and to enable us to serve and glorify Christ together. The eye cannot say it has no need of the ear. If all were hands, how would we walk? Each part of the body is needed to serve the whole. The exercise of our gift is needed to strengthen other saints. We, in turn, will be helped toward maturity through the gifts of others.

Paul told the Romans that he wished to impart some overflow blessing from his gifts to them, in turn receiving strength from them (Rom. 1:11, 12). Another time, Paul used his gift of encouragement to cheer up saddened companions in a harrowing shipwreck; later he needed cheering up himself by Christians who came part way down from Rome to meet him (Acts 27:25; 28:15). We should throw our individual gifts into the common stock so as to receive mutual aid.

Gifts are for the common good, not individual glory. Paul put it this way: "The manifestation of the Spirit is given to every man to profit withal" (1 Cor. 12:7). Spiritual abilities are for the benefit of others, the upbuilding of the church.

The Spirit gave gifts "for the perfecting of the saints, for the work of the ministry, for the edifying of the body of Christ" (Eph. 4:12). This verse seems to indicate that gifts have three purposes, but the punctuation misleads. Both commas interfere with the apostle's meaning. Omit the commas to get the correct sense. Gifts are "for the perfecting of the saints for the work of the ministry for the edifying of the body of Christ." In other words, gifts prepare saints for the task of ministering in order to build up the body of Christ. Restating it, gifts train servants that they may do the Master's work, which will then result in the maturing of the church.

A wrong attitude asks, "Why should I attend church and get involved there? What will I get out of it?" By attendance and involvement, you will minister through your gifts to the good of others. And others will contribute to your spiritual welfare.

A pastor will often invite to his pulpit evangelists, Bible teachers, and other ministers who have gifts differing from his own. This augments his ministry, adding considerably to the edification of his flock.

Dr. John Owen, scholar and Chancellor of Oxford University,

used to go hear John Bunyan, unlearned mender of pots and pans, whenever he came to London. One day King Charles asked Owen, "With all your learning, why do you bother to go to hear that simple Bunyan preach?"

Replied Owen, "Had I the tinker's gifts, I'd gladly relinquish my learning."

The mutual ministry of gifts rules out the lone wolf. No one is gifted enough, wise enough, or strong enough to live apart from others. We should not be parasites nor paralyzed members of the body of Christ.

Use Your Gift—Or Else

The parable of the talents, using financial investments as an illustration, teaches that we shall be held responsible for all our endowments and opportunities—and this includes the use of our gifts, whether one, two, or five.

It behooves us to discover and develop our spiritual abilities. Writing to the Romans, Paul listed seven gifts, urging their faithful exercise, and then added that we should be "fervent in spirit, serving the Lord" (12:11).

Youth is not excused from the exercise of gifts. "Let no man despise thy youth; but be thou an example. . . . Neglect not the gift that is in thee" (1 Tim. 4:12, 14).

Too many Christians, young and old, are content to sit back and let others do the work. An unknown poet has written:

"There's a clever young fellow named Somebody Else—
There's nothing this fellow can't do.
He's busy from morning 'til way late at night
Just substituting for you.

"When asked to do this or asked to do that
So often you're set to reply:
'Get Somebody Else, Mr. Chairman—
He'll do it much better than I.'

"There's so much to do in our parish;
So much, and the workers are few.
And Somebody Else gets weary and worn
Just substituting for you.

"So next time you're asked to do something worthwhile
Come up with this honest reply:
'If Somebody Else can give time and support,
It's obviously true, so can I.' "

The Heidelberg Catechism says, "First, that all and every one who believes, being members of Christ, are in common partakers of Him and of all His riches and gifts; secondly, that every one must know it to be his duty readily and cheerfully to employ his gifts for the advantage and salvation of other members" (Question 55).

Dr. Carl Henry, editor-at-large of *Christianity Today,* wrote, "Each of us has special gifts to exercise spiritual outreach. . . . Let every Bible-believing church suggest its ablest men and women and let no believer escape with the ruse that he or she is vocationally good for nothing to the cause of Christ. No believer is excused" (copyright 1972 by *Christianity Today*).

Each of us should be our unique self. We should find out what we are gifted to do and do our thing. We should not try to imitate somebody else, like some famous evangelist or Bible teacher. We should not quickly condemn someone else's ministry, for the Salvation Army captain and the theological professor may not comprehend each other's dialect, but we should realize there is room for both.

In the day of judgment we'll not be lauded for the magnificence of our mansions, the chrome on our cars, the size of our salaries, the far-and-wideness of our fame. But we will be praised if we can properly respond to the question, "Did you faithfully use the gifts I loaned you?"

Why is the world still so far from being evangelized? Might it be that God has given enough believers the gifts of evangelism and teaching so that long ago all nations should have had opportunity to follow Christ? Might it be that men, women, and youth have just not responded to God's call to discover and use their gifts? Might it be that professing Christians have put their own interests first, neglecting the Great Commission? And might it be that many in the day of judgment will lose a full reward?

When Queen Mary used to visit Balmoral Castle in Scotland every summer, so well-known and beloved was she that she walked unescorted around the countryside. One afternoon, venturing far from home and suddenly noting dark clouds, she stopped at a door to ask to borrow an umbrella.

Not recognizing the queen, the lady of the house was reluctant to lend her brand new umbrella to a stranger. Her cast-off umbrella from the attic had one broken rib and several holes. With an apology, she handed it to the queen.

The next day the lady answered a knock at her door. She opened to a man in gold braid who held a long envelope. "The queen sent me," the stranger said, "and she asked me to thank you for the loan of your umbrella."

For a moment the lady was stunned, then burst into tears. As the courier turned away, he could hear her muttering over and over, "Had I known it was the queen, I'd have given her my best!"

We are all gifted children. And we will answer for it!

Therefore, "As every man hath received the gift, even so minister the same one to another, as good stewards of the manifold grace of God" (1 Peter 4:10).

2

What Is a Gift?

In the early days of radio broadcasting, a California tenor was called the highest paid radio singer. He was so named because he received $25 for singing just one note—the final and top note in a theme song which no one else in the chorus could hit. He possessed a natural gift.

The Apostle Paul stressed the importance of understanding the nature of gifts. He wrote, "Concerning spiritual gifts, brethren, I would not have you ignorant" (1 Cor. 12:1).

Though the word for spiritual gifts in the above verse is *pneumatikon,* literally *spirituals,* referring to the source of gifts as the Holy Spirit, the usual word is *charisma* (plural, *charismata,* as in Rom. 12:6), which means *gift of grace.* The two words are used together in Paul's salutation to the Romans, "I long to see you, that I may impart unto you some *spiritual gift"* (1:11). The word for gift (*charisma*) is derived from the word for grace (*charis*).

People today often speak of *charisma* as a certain charm, magnetism, personality plus, or "it." (A clothing company calls its high-fashion, quality-workmanship shirt *Charisma.* A beauty parlor is named *Charisma.*) But the New Testament gives the word a deeper significance.

A gift has been described as a special qualification granted by the Spirit to every believer to empower him to serve within the framework of the body of Christ.

Someone called a gift a divinely ordained spiritual ability

through which Christ enables His church to execute its task on earth.

Another definition terms gifts "extraordinary endowments bestowed by the Holy Spirit sovereignly and undeservedly on believers as instruments for Christian service and church edification."

These definitions point up certain facts about gifts, including their

source—the special grace of the Holy Spirit;
nature—spiritual ability, endowment, power;
purpose—service, or ministry, to edify saints.

A short, simple definition would be: *a gift is a Spirit-given ability for Christian service.* Examples of gifts will be given in the following chapters.

Gifts Are Not Singular

Sometimes people speak of the "charismatic movement" as though the Spirit's gifts consisted solely of tongues-speaking (perhaps along with miracles and healing). Such limited usage is misleading and unbiblical, for the term *charismatic* should refer to all gifts, at least 18 of which are mentioned by Paul.

The Prairie Overcomer editorialized, "One of the unfortunate results of the contemporary use of the word *charismatic* is the impression that there is only one manifestation of the Spirit, and that the gift of tongues. Yet when the Apostle Paul used the word in any of its various forms, he was referring to many gifts."

The editorial compared those who magnify one gift and neglect the others to a grocer who would speak of his store as a candy emporium. Ordinarily a grocer stocks all the staple food items. Likewise, the Gospel, when properly preached, contains all the essentials of Christian experience.

Paul's opening remarks in the section on the gifts (1 Cor. 12: 1-4) negates their singularity and emphasizes their plurality. Here is an amplification of his thought. "When you were unbelievers, the essence of your religious experience was the feeling of being carried away in the worship of dumb idols. Now, however, as you experience the Holy Spirit, your desire is to honor Jesus in the intelligent and simple ascription of deity to Him. You Corinthians tend to think of the Spirit as revealing Himself only in one way, that of tongues-speaking. You need to learn that the Holy Spirit manifests Himself, not only in rational praise to Jesus, calling

Him Lord, but through varieties of gifts. For there are diversities of gifts."

The gifts are many, not just one.

Gifts Are Not Talents

Non-Christians have talents through common grace, present from birth. Many unbelievers play the piano well, paint beautifully, sculpture realistically, master languages easily, orate eloquently, write effectively. But these are talents, not gifts. No unbeliever has a spiritual gift. Only believers are gifted spiritually.

Talents have to do with techniques and methods; gifts have to do with spiritual abilities. Talents depend on natural power, gifts on spiritual endowment. Speaking of gifts, Peter urges, "If any man speak, let him speak as the oracles of God; if any man minister, let him do it as of the ability which God giveth" (1 Peter 4:11).

Talents instruct, inspire, or entertain on a natural level. Gifts relate to the building up of the saints (or to evangelization). Something supernatural happens in the one who is ministering when a gift is exercised. Nothing supernatural happens in one who is performing when a talent is displayed. And though God may minister His grace, because He is sovereign, even through an unsaved person (who sings a song well, for example), that person has still only shown talent, not a gift.

	Talent	*Gift*
Source:	Common grace of Spirit	Special grace of Spirit
Time Given:	Present from natural birth	Present from new birth
Nature:	Natural ability	Spiritual endowment
Purpose:	Instruction, entertainment, inspiration on a natural level	Spiritual growth of saints; Christian service

Talents and gifts are related. Literary, oratorical, artistic, musical, or linguistic talents may be avenues through which the Holy Spirit will use a person's gifts. But writing, speaking, or vocal abilities are talents, not gifts.

For example, a Christian with a magnificent bass voice sings in secular concerts to the delight and entertainment of thousands. But because this is a natural ability, developed through natural powers and resulting in delighting the hearers, it is a talent, not a gift. A Christian should develop his talents. They may bring inspiration and help in common grace to others. Also the Holy Spirit may choose to use our talents as avenues for the exercise of gifts He may bestow upon us. Should the Spirit not have as fine an avenue as possible for the ministry of the gift?

Suppose to this Christian with the magnificent trained bass voice the Spirit has given the gift of encouragement. Through his singing he can exercise his gift to encourage the saints. If given the gift of evangelism, through his singing he can win people to Christ. Though natural aptitudes are not spiritual gifts, the Spirit may choose to use our natural powers for the exercise of our God-given gifts.

Many old writers suggest that gifts are frequently distributed according to the "conformation which each one has received by nature." Gifts often build on a natural foundation. A person who is by nature a man of vision may be given the gift of faith. A natural-born teacher may be given the gift of teaching. Luke, in addition to his natural abilities in Greek, keen observation, and historical accuracy, was given, among others, the gift of teaching, which utilized these natural aptitudes. Our natural facilities may well point the direction in which our gifts will be used. The Holy Spirit may well express Himself through a man's natural powers.

However, the possession of natural talent doesn't mean God will necessarily choose to use it. Likewise, the Holy Spirit may choose to give a gift to someone lacking natural aptitude in that line. A young man who stuttered seriously told his parents he was called of God to preach. Though they ridiculed and threatened to withhold financial help, he persisted till he became an effective youth evangelist. The Spirit may well assign a gift of preaching to someone without natural speaking ability.

The Spirit may more likely give the gift of preaching to those who do have a talent for speaking. However, caution must be exercised by such lest they depend on their natural ability instead of diligently developing their gift of preaching in dependence on the Spirit.

Someone may ask, "Is teaching a natural talent or a spiritual gift?" For a non-Christian it's a talent. But when that person becomes a Christian, the Spirit may intensify that talent with a supernatural power, heighten, reinforce, and transcend it with a divine plus, to the edification of the saints.

Thus, spiritual gifts by their supernatural source, nature, and purpose, are to be differentiated from natural talents, though often they may be interrelated.

Gifts Are Not Offices

Many offices are mentioned in the New Testament—apostle, prophet, evangelist, pastor, teacher, elder (bishop), and deacon. These offices pertain more to the person, whereas gifts relate to the endowments given the person by the Spirit.

Naturally, a person with an office should have the gift corresponding to that office; otherwise his office would be in name only. A divinely-appointed prophet would have the gift of prophecy, a teacher the gift of teaching, an evangelist the gift of evangelism. However, a person could have the gift belonging to an office without having that office. A man could have the gift of prophecy without being a prophet officially. A believer could have the gift of teaching without having the office of teacher. A person could have the gift of evangelism without being an official evangelist.

Summing up, a believer would not hold a divinely-appointed office without possessing the corresponding gift. But it's likely many Christians possess a gift without appointment to that office. You may well have the gift of shepherding (pastoring) without being called to the office of pastor. You may well have the gift of leading (ruling, government) without holding the office of deacon or elder.

This book will not deal with offices, but will limit itself to discussion of the gifts pertaining to the various offices.

Gifts Are Not Ministries

Gifts must be exercised. The specialty, sphere, or area in which a gift is exercised constitutes a ministry. Thus, a ministry is not a gift, but an outlet for employment of a gift.

The gift of preaching may be exercised to adults, to mass audiences, to radio, on TV, to youth. The gift of teaching may be administered in the formal classroom situation, in visitation, in home Bible studies, in children's meetings, or in a one-to-one personal conversation. For example, older wives are to instruct younger women to love their families and live faithfully (Titus 2:4). These areas of service all represent ministries.

Though a Christian's gifts remain the same, his ministries may change. Paul's locale of work frequently changed, especially on his missionary tours. He moved from place to place—Derbe, Lystra, back to Antioch, Philippi, Athens, Corinth, Ephesus, to name a few. Even prior to his first missionary journey, he carried relief to the famine-stricken brethren in Jerusalem, the completion of which Luke termed fulfilling a ministry (Acts 12:25). Though Paul's gift was to preach the Gospel, his ministry was to the Gentiles (Acts 21:19; Rom. 15:15, 16; Gal. 1:16). However, he did not confine his ministry to the Gentiles but first preached to the Jews, then on their rejection to the Gentiles (Acts 18:4-6; 19:8-10).

Talents—music, writing, linguistics—may be regarded in a sense as ministries through which gifts are employed.

Gifts Are Not Fruit
The gifts of the Spirit differ from the fruit of the Spirit in many ways:

Gifts	Fruit
Have to do with service	Have to do with character (love, joy, peace, etc.; Gal. 5:22, 23)
Are the means to an end	Is the end (Rom. 1:11-13)
What a man has	What a man is
Given from without	Produced from within
In plural	In singular—"but the *fruit*"
All gifts not possessed by every believer	Every variety of fruit should be in every believer
Will cease	Permanent (1 Cor. 13:8-10, *Living Bible*)

Possession of gifts does not indicate godliness of life. Samson continued to perform feats long after he was out of touch with God. Judas, likely one of the 70 who cast out demons, became a betrayer (Luke 10:17). Two quarreling women at Philippi, whom Paul exhorted to make up, had previously exercised gifts with Paul (Phil. 4:2, 3). Though the Corinthians excelled in gifts (1 Cor. 1:7), their church was riddled with problems including divisions, fornication, and drunkenness at the Lord's table. It is possible for a church to be endowed with an abundance of gifts, yet be full of envy, carnality, and discord.

Because it's better to be godly than gifted, Paul positioned his love chapter (1 Cor. 13) right in the middle of his long section dealing with gifts (chaps. 12—14). Without love, gifts are but sounding brass, tinkling cymbal, profitless, nothing. The fruit of the Spirit is much more important than the gifts.

It's possible to have powerful gifts but puny goodness. To win the prize in the Christian race, godliness is required. Paul wrote of the danger of exercising the gift of preaching to others, then himself becoming shelved (1 Cor. 9:24-27).

Analysis of qualifications for the offices of elder and deacon (1 Tim. 3:1-12; Titus 1:6-9) reveals emphasis on the fruit of the Spirit, not gifts. The only gift qualifications seem to be aptness to teach and hospitality. Overwhelmingly necessary are spiritual graces (fruit) like patience, goodness, self-control, humility, love.

Adoniram Judson, pioneer missionary to Burma, answering a question about qualifications for missionaries, wrote, "In regard to the education necessary for missionaries, it appears to me that whatever of mental improvement, or of literary and scientific attainment, is desirable in a minister's home, is desirable in a missionary. I feel, however, more and more, the inadequacy and comparative insignificance of all human accomplishments, whether in a minister or a missionary, and the unspeakable, overwhelming importance of spiritual graces—humility, patience, meekness, love" (*The Life of Adoniram Judson,* Edward Judson, American Baptist Publication Society, Philadelphia, Pa.).

In summary, then, gifts are Spirit-given abilities for Christian service. There is not just one gift, but many. Because of their supernatural source, nature, and purpose, gifts are to be distinguished from natural talents. They are also to be distinguished from office and from ministries. They differ from the *fruit* of the Spirit, and rank lower in importance.

At 5 o'clock one snowy morning, a missionary candidate rang the bell at the address of the missionary examiner's home. He was ushered into the office, where he sat till 8 o'clock for an interview.

The examiner, a retired missionary, began his interrogation.

"Can you spell?"

Rather mystified the candidate answered, "Yes, sir."

"All right; spell *baker*."

"Baker—b-a-k-e-r."

"Fine. Now do you know anything about numbers?" the examiner continued.

"Yes, sir; something."

"Please add two and two."

"Four," replied the candidate.

"That's fine," commented the examiner. "I believe you have passed. I'll tell the board tomorrow."

At the board meeting, the examiner reported on the interview. "He has all the qualifications of a missionary. First, I tested him on self-denial, making him arrive at my house at 5 A.M. He left a warm bed and came out in the snow without any complaint.

"Second, I tested him on promptness. He arrived on time.

"Third, I examined him on patience. I made him wait three hours to see me.

"Fourth, I tested him on temper. He failed to show any sign of aggravation or anger at the delay.

"Fifth, I tried his humility by asking him questions that a seven-year-old child could answer, and he showed no indignation. So, you see, I believe the candidate meets the requirements. He will make the missionary we need."

Spirit-given abilities are necessary; but Spirit-produced fruit is more significant.

3

How Many Gifts?

Someone has imagined the Carpenter's tools holding a conference. Brother Hammer presided. Several suggested he leave the meeting because he was too noisy. Replied the Hammer, "If I have to leave this shop, Brother Screw must go also. You have to turn him around again and again to get him to accomplish anything."

Brother Screw then spoke up. "If you wish, I'll leave. But Brother Plane must leave too. All his work is on the surface. His efforts have no depth."

To this Brother Plane responded, "Brother Rule will also have to withdraw, for he is always measuring folks as though he were the only one who is right."

Brother Rule then complained against Brother Sandpaper, "You ought to leave too because you're so rough and always rubbing people the wrong way."

In the midst of all this discussion, in walked the Carpenter of Nazareth. He had arrived to start His day's work. Putting on His apron, He went to the bench to make a pulpit from which to proclaim the Gospel. He employed the hammer, screw, plane, rule, sandpaper, and all the other tools. After the day's work when the pulpit was finished, Brother Saw arose and remarked, "Brethren, I observe that all of us are workers together with the Lord."

God is a God of variety. In nature, what a diversity of animals! Every snowflake is different, every fingerprint, every face. Likewise, God is a God of variety in His church. What a diversity of gifts He has bestowed on believers to equip them for service!

The Lists of Gifts

In three different chapters in three separate epistles, Paul makes a list of gifts. These gifts vary from list to list, though with some repetition. In the left-hand column below, seven gifts are listed. In the middle column, 13 gifts are listed. They are cataloged in the order in which they make their appearance. The number on the right of some middle-column gifts tells how many times that gift is mentioned in 1 Corinthians 12. In the right-hand column, reference is made to the gift instead of the office. For example, instead of saying *prophet* we use *prophecy;* instead of *evangelist,* we say *evangelism.*

Rom. 12:3-8	*1 Cor. 12:8-10, 28-30*	*Eph. 4:11*
Prophecy	Word of wisdom	Apostleship
Ministering (Helps)	Word of knowledge	Prophecy
Teaching	Faith	Evangelism
Exhorting	Healing (3)	Pastoring
Giving	Miracles (3)	Teaching
Government (Ruling)	Prophecy (3)	
Showing Mercy	Discernment	
	Tongues (3)	
	Interpretation (2)	
	Apostleship (2)	
	Teaching (2)	
	Ministration (Helps)	
	Government (Ruling)	

Prophecy and teaching are the only gifts to appear in all three lists. Apostleship, ministration (helps) and government (ruling) are found in two lists. Thirteen gifts are mentioned in only one list. A total of *18 different* gifts are cataloged.

Complete or Incomplete?

Is the above list of 18 gifts exhaustive? Are all the gifts included? Or are there some gifts not found in these listings? Is the list perhaps only suggestive?

Many believe the catalog is far from complete. As not all the members of the human body are mentioned in 1 Corinthians 12, but only the ear, eye, hand, and foot, so all the gifts for the body of Christ are not included in these listings, it is argued. Some reason further that since each of the individual inventories contains a suggestive, partial enumeration of gifts, then the sum total of the three groupings may well provide an incomplete listing as well.

The well-known Bible teacher Dr. G. Campbell Morgan, in a foreword to a volume of poems by Edith Hickman Divall published in 1906, indicated his conviction that the catalog was not comprehensive.

"In the Scriptures of the New Covenant we find different lists of the 'gifts' bestowed upon His church by the risen and glorified Lord. It has often been pointed out that no two of these lists are exactly alike. There is deep suggestiveness and great beauty in this fact. We are all strangely prone to mechanism, and are too fond of tabulating and stating systematically even the things of God. There would have been some sort of satisfaction in having an exhaustive list of His gifts. Yet how sad would it have been, for inevitably we should have spent much time in seeking to place each other by our gifts, or pitying such as seemed to possess none. The gifts were never tabulated exhaustively because they cannot be exhausted; and while today some of the earliest are not found, many new and precious ones are ours" (*Prairie Overcomer,* Three Hills, Alberta, Canada).

F. W. Robertson comments, "God has given to one man eloquence, to another businesslike habits, to some exquisitely fine feelings, to others a more blunted feeling, for even that is a gift, without which some duties could not be suitably performed" (*Expository Lectures on the Corinthians,* Kegan Paul, Trench & Co., London, England).

Regarding the "gifts" mentioned in the preceding paragraph, would not *eloquence* qualify more as a talent than gift? Also, would not the gift of blunted feeling (which would permit a missionary to scrape an ugly ulcer on a national's leg) be considered part of the gift of showing mercy?

One widely-held view is that every possible gift for the church could be classified under one of the gifts in Paul's three tabulations. Thus, though all the gifts in the church are not actually specified in Scripture, yet every unnamed, genuine gift could be subsumed under one of the listed gifts.

In this view, each of Paul's specific gifts becomes an umbrella which shelters a group of related gifts. This concept proposes that, though all the offspring are not specifically recorded, all the parent-gifts are named in the Pauline tabulations. In the sense of offspring registration, the New Testament is suggestive and incomplete; in the sense of parent nomenclature Paul's lists are practically exhaustive and complete.

The abilities to do Jewish soul-winning, to operate a rescue mission, to visit and witness to newcomers, would all be classified under the gift of evangelism.

Another example of a gift not mentioned in Paul's three series but potentially classifiable under one in his listings is hospitality. On what grounds should hospitality be considered a gift? When Peter urges every believer to minister his gift, what led him to that exhortation was the concept of hospitality. Note the close proximity between *hospitality* and *gift*. "Use hospitality one to another without grudging. As every man hath received the gift, even so minister the same one to another" (1 Peter 4:9, 10). From thinking of a gift in particular, Peter easily shifts into gifts in general. Because of this contextual relationship, hospitality will be considered a gift worthy of separate treatment in a later chapter. But note that hospitality is logically and easily subsumed under a larger class, the gift of ministration or helps.

Through the years, other abilities have been frequently mentioned as deserving recognition as gifts along with those on Paul's lists. Three, especially, keep cropping up. First, celibacy is termed a gift by Paul (1 Cor. 7:7). Though Paul wishes all were unmarried, he calls for tolerance, acknowledging that people could be celibate only if they had that proper gift from God. Perhaps celibacy should be called a gift, but because many regard it more an ability by nature, it is omitted from most lists. Whether or not a gift, celibacy should be more often considered as a valid alternative lifestyle to marriage.

The second is martyrdom. In showing the superiority of love over gifts such as tongues, prophecy, knowledge, faith, showing mercy—which all are bona fide gifts listed somewhere in his three tabulations—Paul mentions the act of martyrdom, not found in the listings. "Though I bestow all my goods to feed the poor, and though I give my body to be burned, and have not charity, it profiteth me nothing" (1 Cor. 13:3).

It is difficult to see how martyrdom, which could be exercised only once, should be considered a gift—unless one refers to a spirit of martyrdom which gives grace for every suffering inflicted by persecutors including death. Or may Paul be extending the thought of the first part of the verse, "bestowing all my goods to feed the poor," to its ultimate self-sacrifice, which would be the giving of one's life? Some do list martyrdom among the gifts, citing, "Unto you it is given . . . not only to believe on Him, but also to suffer for His sake" (Phil. 1:29).

The third sometimes-suggested gift is missionary endowment. C. Peter Wagner, well-known church growth authority, says in *Frontiers of Missionary Strategy* (Moody Press, Chicago, Ill.) that the missionary gift should be added to the list, though not specifically mentioned in the New Testament. The missionary gift will be included in the following listing, but under the term *apostleship,* as the continuing ability of an extinct office.

Classification of Gifts

Admittedly, the gifts have been classified in many ways. We shall attempt our own groupings.

One word which best characterizes the function of all the gifts is *ministering.* But under the general function of *ministering,* the gifts divide into two major types, *speaking* and *serving,* as stated by Peter, "Whoever speaks, let him speak as it were the utterances of God; whoever serves, let him do so as by the strength which God supplies" (1 Peter 4:11, *New American Standard Bible*).

	Ministering	
Speaking	*Serving*	*Signifying*
Apostleship *	Ministration (Helps)	Miracles
Prophecy	—Hospitality	Healing
Evangelism	Giving	Tongues
Pastoring	Government (Ruling)	Interpretation
Teaching	Showing mercy	
Exhorting	Faith	
Word of Wisdom	Discernment	
Word of Knowledge	Miracles	
Tongues	Healing	
Interpretation		

To the two major groups we add a third. Four gifts, the last two in each of the speaking and serving groups also qualify as *sign* gifts (see chart above). The New Testament frequently speaks of miracles, wonders, and signs. The gifts of miracles, healing, and tongues all possessed sign value in apostolic times. The

---

* Missionary

sign gifts are not cataloged in either the Roman or Ephesian epistles, only in the first letter to Corinth, where one of the sign gifts was causing problems. Also, the sign gifts have an authenticating relationship to the apostles (2 Cor 12:12; Heb. 2:3, 4).

Beginning with the next chapter, each gift will be discussed in the order in which it appears in the preceding listing. Paul does not give us a definite hierarchical ranking of gifts, though he does seem to put apostleship, prophecy, and teaching above miracles, healings, helps, government, and tongues (1 Cor. 12:28). He definitely rates prophecy superior to tongues (1 Cor. 14:1-5).

Interpretation
With *hospitality* considered separately, though it could be listed under the gift of *ministration* or *helps,* the list now numbers 19.

Gifts overlap. This makes it difficult to separate some gifts completely from others. Certainly, prophecy incorporates some teaching. Evangelism also has some content of teaching. The gifts of helps (ministration) and of showing mercy are related. Several gifts seem to shade into each other.

No gift is restricted to either sex. All gifts are for both men and women. Even in groups which forbid woman pastors, some women need the gift of pastoring in order to shepherd other women and children who might need their care. Women also require the gift of teaching to instruct other women and children. The gift of government is essential for those in places of leadership in women's groups.

Absence of Gifts Does Not Excuse Disobedience to Commands
Many gifts operate in the area of clear-cut commands. For example, the Christian is commanded to liberality in giving. Because a believer does not have the gift of giving, he cannot say, "Never pass me the plate any more. I don't need to tithe, nor even give, for I do not have that gift." All believers are ordered to support the Lord's work financially. Though some may be given a special ability to donate generously to the Lord's work, all are to share.

All are commanded to witness. Because a person does not possess the gift of evangelism is no excuse for failure to evangelize. Some will be given a special endowment for evangelism, but all are enjoined to share their faith.

Because a believer has not the gift of prophecy, he cannot refuse to spread the Word as opportunity arises. When the saints were scattered out of Jerusalem throughout all the region of Judea and Samaria, they "went everywhere preaching the Word" (Acts 8:4). Many doubtless did not have the gift of prophecy, but all spoke forth for Christ.

Though a Christian may not have the gift of discernment, he is commanded to "prove all things," to "hold fast that which is good" (1 Thes. 5:21).

If a saint does not possess the gift of showing mercy, he is not exempt from comforting the feeble-minded (1 Thes. 5:14) and assisting widows and the fatherless (James 1:27).

Though commands cover most areas of gifts, they do not seem to pertain to the signifying gifts. A pastor was asked why he did not encourage miracles, healing, and tongues in his congregation. After honest heart-searching he concluded that he should not promote these sign gifts because, as he read the New Testament to practice its commands, he had not found any specific orders to do these things. He could not think of any definite verse urging the believer to perform miracles or healings, or to seek to speak in tongues.

But commands cover almost every other area of gifts. Review the list of gifts in the *speaking* and *serving* columns, and note how the area of most gifts is penetrated by New Testament commands. In fact, it is as we do service by obedience to commands that we begin to discover special abilities in certain spheres. Moreover, it is our responsibility both to discover and develop whatever our gifts may be. But even if we don't have a divine plus in a particular area, we are still obliged to obey commands in that sphere.

Someone has likened Christians to ballplayers on a team. Every member of the lineup is expected to take his turn at bat and do his best to get on base. Though some may make their major contribution in some other way such as pitching or fielding, all are expected to try to get a hit. Two or three players may have the ability to hit the long ball, but all members of the team try to single their way on base.

On the Christian team, every believer is expected to try to connect in every area of Christian living. True, some believers may have special abilities in certain areas, but this does not excuse every believer from taking his turn at the plate and doing his best. Every believer must witness, show mercy, give, and obey every command, though only some may have Spirit-given endowments for particular Christian services.

Sufficient gifts have been bestowed by the Holy Spirit to meet every need of the church. Here are some examples of needs with at least one corresponding gift that answers that need:

for preaching the Word	—the gift of prophecy
for instruction	—the gift of teaching
for encouragement	—the gift of exhortation
for doing kindness	—the gift of showing mercy
for financial support	—the gift of giving
for enablement, power	—the gift of faith
for protection	—the gift of discernment
for reaching the lost	—the gift of evangelism

The Holy Spirit knows which gifts are needed, and when and where. The church cannot prosper unless those needed are functioning in their place.

A man broke his left arm. One night when he couldn't sleep, he imagined a dialogue between his right and left hand. The right hand said, "Left hand, you are not missed. Everybody's glad that it was you that was broken and not me. You are not very important."

The left hand said, "How are you superior?"

Said the right hand, "Why, my owner cannot write a letter without me."

The left answered, "But who holds the paper on which he writes?"

Said the right, "Who wields the hammer?"

Said the left, "Who holds the nail that the hammer hits?"

Asked the right, "Who guides the plane when the carpenter smooths a board?"

Retorted the left, "Who steadies the board?"

Said the right, "When our owner walks down the street and lifts his hat to greet someone, which of us does it?"

Replied the left, "Who holds his briefcase while he does it?"

Then the left continued, "Let me ask you a question, When our owner shaved yesterday he used you, but his face is cut because I wasn't there to help. Also our owner's watch has stopped. Know why? You may do the winding, but if I'm not there to hold it, the watch won't get wound. You cannot take money out of the wallet because I'm not there to hold it. The master can do very few things without me."

Similarly, our divine Master needs all the members of His body to exercise all their gifts so that His body may function smoothly and effectively.

Part II
The
Speaking
Gifts

4

The Apostolic Gift

Two young seminary students spent the summer before their graduation as short-term missionaries in Taiwan. Good friends, they had often discussed whether or not the Lord wanted them on the mission field. Now they decided to spend three months to see how they acclimated.

One enjoyed his stint to the hilt. He adapted readily to the culture. He never got sick. He learned snatches of the language. The time flew by.

The second prospective missionary hated the food, learned only a few words of the language, became ill three different times, and wanted to spend most of his time with the Americans rather than with the nationals. At the end he exclaimed, "I never want to be a missionary." His companion could hardly wait to apply to the missionary board to return after his final seminary year.

For years Christian people spoke of the missionary call. Increasingly today, they talk of the missionary gift, which involves communicating the Gospel transculturally. Also, more than ever, many are identifying the missionary gift with the apostolic gift.

First on our list of spiritual abilities is the apostolic gift. The word *apostle* occurs approximately 75 times in the New Testament, in 19 of the 27 books. Because it refers to an office that died out when the apostles passed away, many exclude it from the list of gifts. Dr. John Stott, well-known Anglican cleric and Bible teacher, says it is one of the gifts that does not exist in the church today. On the other hand, many believe the gift did not die out.

For example, John Calvin wrote that God raised up apostles "on particular occasions, when required by the necessity of the times," and "as He has done in our own time" (*Institutes of the Christian Religion*, Book IV, Chapter II, Presbyterian Board of Christian Education, Philadelphia, Pa.).

Did the gift die out? Or is it a continuing gift today?

Perhaps the answer is "yes" to both questions, if *apostle* has a two-fold aspect. In its restricted usage, the office has finished; in its broader phase, the gift still functions. Officially, the apostolate ended with the apostles; unofficially, the apostolic gift persists to our day as the missionary gift.

The Restricted, Official Usage

In several ways the apostles were unique.

1. They had been with Jesus from the beginning.

When Peter listed qualifications for a replacement for Judas, he said, "Wherefore of these men which have companied with us all the time that the Lord Jesus went in and out among us, beginning from the baptism of John . . ." (Acts 1:21, 22).

2. They had a personal call from Christ.

The Lord chose twelve "that they should be with Him, and that He might send them forth to preach" (Mark 3:14). He commissioned them, "As My Father hath sent Me, even so send I you" (John 20:21).

3. They were witnesses of the resurrection.

Peter, in listing an apostle's qualifications, said that he must "be a witness with us of His resurrection" (Acts 1:22).

4. They laid the doctrinal foundation of the church.

Jesus had promised them, "The Holy Ghost, whom the Father will send in My name, He shall teach you all things, and bring all things to your remembrance, whatsoever I have said unto you. . . . When He, the Spirit of truth, is come, He will guide you into all truth: for He shall not speak of himself; . . . and He will shew you things to come" (John 14:26; 16:13). The major fulfillment of this promise was the New Testament revelation inspired by the Holy Spirit. Later-century Christians admitted to the sacred canon only those writings which they knew emanated from the apostolic circle, or from their close associates such as Mark, Luke, and James, the brother of Jesus. The test of New Testament canonicity was apostolicity.

5. *They laid the structural foundation of the church.*

This involved the use of the keys (Matt. 16:18, 19) in opening the door for the Gospel to Jews, (Acts 2:38-41), to half-Jewish Samaritans (Acts 8:14-17), and to Gentiles (Acts 10:44-48). The church was built upon the foundation of the apostles and prophets (Eph. 2:20).

6. *They had power to work miracles.*

After Pentecost, "many wonders and signs were done by the apostles" (Acts 2:43). Three chapters later we read, "And by the hands of the apostles were many signs and wonders wrought among the people" (5:12). Another three chapters later we are told "that through laying on of the apostles' hands the Holy Ghost was given" (8:18). The purpose of this miraculous power was to authenticate the apostolic witness (2 Cor. 12:12; Heb. 2:4). A major segment of the church holds that when the apostles died the sign gifts diminished dramatically or disappeared.

7. *They will one day sit on 12 thrones judging the 12 tribes of Israel* (Luke 22:29, 30). *Also their names will be inscribed on the 12 foundations of the New Jerusalem* (Rev. 21:14).

The apostles were unique in these ways. The word *apostle* had an official usage limited to the Twelve (Acts 9:27; 1 Cor. 15:7). No one of a later generation could meet their qualifications. Thus there could never be any such thing as apostolic successors. The office could not be repeated nor transmitted. When the apostles died, the office of apostleship died with them. Those who made false claim to this office were called liars (Rev. 2:2).

But persons beyond the circle of the Twelve were termed apostles, which leads us to consider the continuing aspect of the apostolic gift. C. Peter Wagner, church growth researcher, in *Frontiers in Missionary Strategy*, holds there is a missionary gift which might well be added to the New Testament lists of gifts. We will position the missionary gift here as the continuing and unofficial phase of the apostolic gift.

The Broader, Unofficial Sense

Others, outside the Twelve, were called apostles:

Barnabas (Acts 14:4, 14)

James, the Lord's brother (Gal. 1:19)

Silas (Silvanus) and Timothy (1 Thes. 1:1; 2:6)

Andronicus and Junia are mentioned as "of note among the

apostles" (Rom. 16:7). Possibly these two were counted among the apostles. More likely, they were considered notable by the apostles, and were not apostles.

The supreme example of a person being called an apostle who was not among the Twelve is, of course, the Apostle Paul (Rom. 1:1). So strong is Paul's claim to being an apostle that Bible interpreters have frequently suggested that the 11 apostles acted too hastily in selecting a replacement for Judas. Had they waited, they claim, the Lord would have revealed Paul as the choice.

Though the validity of Matthias' appointment has been questioned often, many facts seem to favor its sanction. In calling for a successor to Judas, Peter grounded his action in Old Testament prophecies. Though not mentioned by name, Matthias evidently acted with the other eleven (Acts 2:14; 6:2; 9:27; 1 Cor. 15:5, 7). The validity of the appointment never seems to have been questioned by the apostles or the church. It is likely that Matthias will be one of the Twelve judging the 12 tribes and that his name, not Paul's, will be inscribed on the foundations of the New Jerusalem.

Though Paul emphatically claimed to be an apostle and appointed so by the Lord, he never makes the claim of having been numbered with the Twelve. Though he was a witness of the risen Christ and did receive special revelations, he did not qualify for apostleship in its restricted, official sense, for he did not accompany Christ in His earthly ministry at any time, much less from the baptism of John. To claim Paul as one of the Twelve is to do violence to the Scriptural qualifications for that office.

When Paul was converted on the Damascus Road, the Lord did not appoint him to be numbered with the Twelve. Nor did Paul ever act as one of the Twelve. Rather he recognized the Twelve in the position which they occupied (1 Cor. 15:5, 7). When he met the apostles in Jerusalem, there is not the slightest suggestion that he considered himself as numbered with the Twelve.

In his thought-provoking and comprehensive volume, *The New Testament Order for Church and Missionary,* author Alexander Rattray Hay points out that when Paul wrote, "Am I not an apostle?" (1 Cor. 9:1-5), he is not making claim to be one of the Twelve, but simply presenting his credentials as a *missionary*, and to having performed the task of a *missionary* in the founding of the church at Corinth (published by New Testament Missionary Union, Audubon, N.J.).

The missionary gift is the continuing aspect of the apostleship. Moreover, suggests Hay, "Paul's ministry and that of his companions is recorded in detail because he and they provide the typical example for the exceedingly important permanent ministry of church-planting. Paul belongs entirely to the church dispensation. He had not been with the Lord prior to the Cross. His conversion, call, and training took place after Pentecost. He is the example of what Christ, indwelling the Church by His Spirit, purposes to do through the Church in this dispensation. The Twelve were a Jewish company with their roots in Judaism. But Paul and his fellow church-planters were purely of the Church, composed of men called, prepared, brought together and led by the Spirit, and it is to them that first place is given in the record of the extension throughout the world of the church that was founded by the Twelve. The fact that Paul was not numbered with the Twelve does not detract from the importance of his ministry; on the contrary, it greatly increases its significance to the church today."

In the early ministry of the twelve apostles, the restricted and broader aspects of their office blended as they presided at the laying of the doctrinal and structural foundation of the first church at Jerusalem and its extension to Samaritans and Gentiles. As the record proceeds, their narrower, official function decreases. No longer together, with special mission fulfilled, they scatter to perform the broader, itinerant, missionary ministry, establishing congregations in regions beyond. The last mention of the apostles being gathered in any official capacity concerns the first church council at Jerusalem (Acts 15:2-6, 23; 16:4). In the first dozen chapters of Acts, the Twelve are prominent; afterward it is Paul and his missionary teams that occupy the scene. Doubtless, during the period covered by the last half of Acts, the dispersed Twelve exercised the same missionary gift as Paul, making church-planting tours to various parts of the known world.

The International Standard Bible Encyclopedia (in an article titled "Ministry") sums up, "In the New Testament and in the other literature of the early church, the word 'apostle' is used in a narrower and in a wider sense. The wider use of the word has descended to the present day; 'apostles' or 'holy apostles' is still the name for missionaries in some parts of the Greek church."

Nature of the Missionary Gift Today

The word *missionary* covers a broad meaning in our day, sometimes losing significance by including almost anyone in Christian service or with Christian concern. One church bulletin carried this filler: "A missionary is a person who never gets used to the thud of heathen feet on the way to eternity."

More accurately, the Random House Dictionary defines a missionary as "a person sent by a church into an area, especially a newly-settled region or foreign country, to carry on evangelism or other activities." Three major concepts in this dictionary definition are found in this simpler statement: a missionary is one *sent* to minister *transculturally* with *church-planting* goals.

1. Sent

The late Isaac Page, missionary to China, used to pun that the meaning of *missionary* also gave his financial status—one cent (sent).

The word *missionary* is rooted in the Latin "to send," while the word *apostle* comes from the Greek "to send." Linguistically, missionary and apostle are equals. Both are *sent* ones.

The missionary is *sent* from, as opposed to being *called* to, a particular church. When Dr. Alan Redpath was called from England to the pastorate of Moody Memorial Church, this did not make him a missionary. Nor did Billy Graham's holding of meetings in Korea at the invitation of the evangelical churches there make him a missionary. Crossing geographical lines does not make a missionary. Rather than being invited *to* a certain area, he is ordered (commissioned) *out of* his original homeland. His destination may not even be specific and definite when he embarks.

The missionary gift may involve working oneself out of a job, staying a few years in one place, then moving to the next. The whole world is the field. C. T. Studd missionaried in three lands: China, India, and Africa.

Incidentally, the double function of the apostle is found in the *Didache,* or *Teaching of the Twelve.* The title refers to the narrow, restricted, official usage—just the Twelve. One section of the book mentions itinerant missionaries as apostles, "Concerning apostles and prophets, so do ye according to the ordinance of the Gospel. Let every apostle, when he cometh to you, be received as the Lord; but he shall not abide more than a single day, or if there be need, a second likewise; but if he abide three days, he is a false prophet" (11:3). Since this book is dated at the beginning of the second century when all the official Twelve had already passed on, the word *apostle* must refer to the continuing missionary gift.

Calvin said that the title of apostles had to be given the Twelve to distinguish them in a peculiar way as announcers of a new and unheard message. Then he added, "according to the meaning and etymology of the word, all the ministers of the Church may be called apostles, because they are all sent by the Lord, and are His messengers" (*Institutes,* Book IV, chapter III). Note the words *sent by the Lord.* But there's more to a missionary than being sent. He must be sent across cultural borders.

2. Transculturally

A pastor on a round-the-world trip to observe missionary work noticed time and again in many countries that he was the object of curious gaze. Especially did people stare at his blonde wife. The couple enjoyed retreating at close of day to some American hotel in major cities, declaring, "We can stand the cultural shock during the day if we can get back to a little bit of American food and life each evening."

Ability to serve in another culture is part of the missionary gift. Not every person who is called "missionary" fits this qualification. Ralph Winter in *Evangelical Missions Quarterly* (1970:55) suggests a three-fold classification of a missionary, only two of which are genuinely eligible for the title. He calls them: M-1, M-2, and M-3.

M-1 is an intracultural ministry as when a young lady travels half-way round the globe to teach in a missionaries' children's school in Taiwan, or when an American pastor spends five years as shepherd of an English-speaking congregation in Saigon. Since neither has to learn a new language, no missionary gift is needed.

M-2 is an interdialectal ministry, as when a missionary goes from the U.S.A. to France. Since he must learn a new language even though the new culture differs minimally from his homeland, the missionary gift is a requisite.

M-3 is intercultural ministry in the extreme sense, as when a missionary settles in Jordan after growing up in the U.S.A. The difficult new language and the radically strange culture demand a missionary gift of the highest order. The home missionary to the inner city would be included somewhere in these last two categories, for often the culture is drastically different, and more often than not, a new language has to be learned.

The missionary gift never comes alone. Other gifts are needed for effective overseas service, like teaching and evangelism and helps. But the missionary gift will enable the person to use these gifts transculturally. If no missionary gift exists, the person will have to employ his gifts in his own familiar culture. The believer with the gift of evangelism, but minus the missionary ability, will have to evangelize in his own culture. To witness competently across cultural lines mandates the missionary gift. Wherever a cultural gap exists, the missionary gift is needed if that person is to survive the strange environment, remain on the field, and do an effective piece of work.

Numerous missionary casualties have resulted from lack of ability to minister cross-culturally. In earlier decades with slow transportation few could test the gift in advance. But today with ease of world-wide travel a person can easily spend time in another culture. A short term on some mission field is an excellent way to probe the transcultural gift. A directory published in 1973 by *Short Terms Abroad*, Wheaton, Ill., lists needs for over 5,000 people to fill jobs, most of which are overseas.

Since every believer does not possess the missionary gift, the slogan that every Christian must find a substitute if he does not go as a missionary is misleading. Just because a Christian doesn't have the gift of teaching doesn't require him to find someone to sub for him as a teacher.

Chapter two ends with the story of a candidate accepted by the examiner for a missionary board because he evidenced the fruit of the Spirit, so necessary for missionary service: self-denial, patience, and humility. But a missionary needs more than Spirit-produced Christlikeness. He also needs the Spirit-given gift of working across cultural borders.

The twelve apostles, after some years in Jerusalem, went transcultural. Had they not been commanded to take the Gospel to all cultures? *Foxe's Book of Martyrs* lists widespread areas where some of the Twelve labored before their deaths. For example:

Upper Asia and Asia Minor—Philip
Ethiopia and Parthia—Matthew
Asia, Edessa—Andrew
Rome—Peter

Edessa—Thaddeus
India—Bartholomew and Thomas
Africa—Simon the Zealot
Asia Minor—John

3. Church-planting goals

Connection with a missionary society plus travel beyond cultural boundaries doesn't make one a missionary. In addition, he must minister with evangelistic goals.

Full-orbed evangelism includes conversion, baptism, growth, and the organized fellowship; in other words, church-planting. The missionary gift calls for the starting of new churches by evangelization of new areas. It is Paul's principle of striving to preach the Gospel, "not where Christ was named, lest I should build upon another man's foundation" (Rom. 15:20). Paul called himself the foundation-layer of the Corinthian church (1 Cor. 3:10).

In the measure that doctors, nurses, linguists, builders, teachers, and helpers contribute to the planting of churches, in that measure do they employ the missionary gift. The missionary is a person engaged in a formalized, structured program of church-planting rather than a casual, hit-or-miss situation.

One writer says that apostles, both the Twelve and post-apostolic, "had one distinguishing characteristic: They had chosen as their life-work to be the missionary pioneers of the Gospel of the Kingdom of Christ. They were engaged in aggressive work, and were distinguished from others, not so much by what they were as by what they did. They were wandering with no fixed place of residence. The requirements of their work might make them abide for long periods in some center, but they had no permanent home life. As the earlier decades passed, their numbers increased rather than diminished" (*I.S.B.E.* p. 2058).

Dr. Ray C. Stedman says, "The apostolic gift is still being given today, though in a secondary sense. It is part of the apostolic gift to start new churches. We call those who do this 'pioneer missionaries' today."

A few outstanding examples of men with the missionary gift in recent centuries are:

William Carey of India,
Adoniram Judson of Burma,
Hudson Taylor of China,
David Livingstone of Africa,

plus a host of lesser-known lights whose names will be blazoned forth in eternity, many of whom have spoken from your pulpit and are supported by your church.

Years ago, before China was engulfed by Communism, the board of directors of a large American company wanted to secure a well qualified man to handle their business interests in China. He had to be not only conversant with the language but familiar with the customs. Also, he had to be a man of tact, strong personality, and administrative ability. They would be willing to pay a large salary.

One of the directors immediately spoke up. "I know just the man you want. Moreover he's already in China, knows their customs, and speaks Chinese fluently. His present salary is just $600 a year, which isn't his fault, but the fault of the board employing him." The directors voted that this member locate and interview personally the man so highly recommended, and to hire him even if necessary to offer a salary as high as $20,000 a year.

After some months of traveling, the director located his man, a missionary, in a remote, interior part of China. He told the missionary of his board's action and informed him how eager the firm was to secure his services. Would he be willing to accept the job for a salary of $10,000?

The missionary shook his head.

"Well, then, would $12,000 be an inducement?"

Again the missionary declined.

"I've come a long way, and I shouldn't go back without some positive news. Will you accept the position for $15,000?"

"No."

"We have no other person in mind. Will you accept for a salary of $20,000?"

The missionary responded with a decisive no.

"Why not?" asked the visitor. "Isn't the salary big enough?"

"To be sure it is," replied the missionary. "In fact, the salary is far larger than the work would justify. The trouble is not with the salary, but with the job. The job isn't big enough!"

What a thrilling job for someone with the missionary gift, sent out to a different culture somewhere around the world, to be engaged in the planting of churches!

5

The Gift of Prophecy

For years, in Washington, Jeanne Dixon has been making predictions. She foretold the assassination of John F. Kennedy four years before he was elected president, the airplane death of Dag Hammarskjold, the Communist takeover of China, and Eisenhower's heart attack and recovery. Is this what is meant by the gift of prophecy? (Note that she made many predictions that did not come true, such as the outbreak of World War III in 1958, Richard Nixon's defeat of John F. Kennedy in the 1960 presidential election, and the admission of Red China to the United Nations in 1959.)

A preacher declares from his pulpit that Russia and the United States will meet headlong in massive battle at Armageddon in our lifetime. Is this what is meant by the gift of prophecy?

The Gift of Prophecy in Bible Times

Usually people think of prediction when they hear the word *prophecy*. But foretelling the future is just a small part of the meaning of prophecy. The English word *prophet* comes from a Greek word composed of two parts which mean literally—*forth-tell*. A prophet is a forth-teller. Among the many messages he tells forth may be some pertaining to the future. Thus forth-telling may involve some foretelling, but only incidentally. The main meaning of prophesying is forth-telling.

Prophecy is forth-telling for another. When God called Moses to deliver Israel out of Egypt, Moses objected on the grounds he could not speak well. Angry, God answered, "Is not Aaron the Levite thy brother? I know that he can speak well . . . Thou shalt speak unto him, and put words in his mouth . . . and he shall be thy spokesman unto the people; and he shall be . . . to thee instead of a mouth . . . and Aaron thy brother shall be thy prophet" (Ex. 4:14-16; 7:1). Aaron, forth-speaking for Moses, became his prophet.

A prophet of God was God's spokesman. The Old Testament includes the writings of prophets, both major and minor, from Moses to Malachi. These men didn't merely foretell the future but rather did forth-tell God's message, which concerned past and present as well as future.

The prophet received a revelation from God by dream, vision, or verbal communication. He then declared that revelation as a messenger in the special service of God. What the Lord put in his mouth he spoke. He acted consciously, not in some trance. He often used a graphic object lesson to emphasize the message.

The Old Testament prophet has been called the "ministerial monitor" of the people. His message was primarily reformative. Prophecies analyzed the current condition and the consequence of continuance in that course, then counseled repentance. Watching out for the spiritual interests of his hearers, the prophet reminded of the Mosaic Law, restated divine commands, and warned of judgment to come.

Prophets instructed, warned, exhorted, promised, rebuked. They protested the mere formalism of perfunctorily offering sacrifices without obedience. They stressed moral duty, promoted righteousness, thundered coming terror on the wicked, and repeated God's gracious promises for the future.

Though the future was often part of their prophetic utterance, their emphasis was historical, practical, and relevant to contemporary conditions, such as when they warned Israel and Judah of the coming Assyrian and Babylonian invasions, plus the doom and desolation that would follow. John the Baptist exercised a prophetic ministry when he admonished Herod that he should not have taken his brother's wife.

First mention of prophets in the New Testament occurs in Acts 11:27, 28: "And in these days came prophets from Jerusalem unto Antioch. And there stood up one of them named Agabus, and signified by the Spirit that there should be great dearth throughout all the world: which came to pass in the days of Claudius Caesar."

Agabus again appears in the record when he warned Paul of persecution if he continued his journey to the Holy City. Taking Paul's girdle and graphically binding the apostle's hands and feet, the prophet said, "Thus saith the Holy Ghost, So shall the Jews at Jerusalem bind the man that owneth this girdle, and shall deliver him into the hands of the Gentiles" (Acts 21:11).

Though the predictive element is paramount in both Agabus' prophecies, most references to New Testament prophets do not stress or even mention a futuristic message.

The church at Antioch in Syria had "certain prophets and teachers" (Acts 13:1). Five names follow.

Conveying the decrees of the first church council to the Gentile believers in Antioch, "Judas and Silas, being prophets also themselves, exhorted the brethren with many words, and confirmed them" (Acts 15:32).

Philip the evangelist "had four daughters, virgins, which did prophesy" (Acts 21:9).

In the Corinthian church, prophecy seemed to be the delivery of an inspired message or revelation for the purpose of edifying (1 Cor. 14:3, 4).

Paul wrote that the church was "built upon the foundation of the apostles and prophets" (Eph. 2:20). That these were Paul's contemporaries, not Old Testament prophets, seems likely from their association with apostles (who are New Testament) and from their location after apostles (instead of "prophets and apostles," the expected order if Old Testament prophets were meant). Besides, prophets mentioned in following chapters (3:5 and 4:11) unmistakably are New Testament prophets. Thus, the Ephesian epistle clearly mentions prophets of the new dispensation three times.

Paul commands the Thessalonians, "Despise not prophesyings" (1 Thes. 5:20).

In the first century, before the New Testament writings were completed, revelations and special messages containing predictions like those of Agabus concerning coming events (famine and Pauline persecution) were given people with the prophetic gift. But what about since the apostolic message has been inscripturated? Does God, in our time, give specific instructions about people, places, and things? Does the prophetic gift today include special, definite, extra-biblical predictions?

What About the Gift of Prophecy in Our Day?

Some hold that prophecy today involves special messages from God, beyond what is found in Scripture, giving guidance regarding job, family, health, and social problems. A few begin their alleged prophetic utterances, "I announce . . . I, the Lord, declare . . ." Some assert that prophecy is poetry of the Spirit, raising thoughts in these predictions above the level of the ordinary and clothing them with beauty of language.

Dangers inhere in this view. Is it then possible for some today to get a prophecy regarding the fluctuations of the stock market, or the weather, or current events as Jeanne Dixon claims?

To protect against rampant and irresponsible forecasts those who hold the view that special predictive messages are possible today insist that prophecies must be confirmed by people of wisdom and spiritual maturity. Wouldn't a wiser and surer check be the inerrant, infallible Word of God, rather than errant, fallible people, spiritual though they may be?

God's revelation has been finished. The Bible is our all-sufficient guide today. Until the completion of the New Testament, during the apostolic age, prophets gave necessary special revelations and reliable guidance. Since the completion of the Bible, in which divine revelation is once-for-all written, the gift of prophecy is now identified with proclamation based on God's Word.

Inspiration at the level at which infallible Scripture was given ended with the completion of the canon. Any prophecy today must of necessity be the unfolding of the significance of that completed message. A. H. Strong, a noted Baptist theologian, wrote that since Christ's ascension prophetic activity is carried on through the preaching of His apostles and ministers, and by the enlightening influence of His Holy Spirit. He said:

"The church is, in a derivative sense, a prophetic institution, established to teach the world by its preaching ordinances. But Christians are prophets only as being proclaimers of Christ's teaching. All modern prophecy that is true is but the republication of Christ's message—the proclamation and expounding of truth already revealed in Scripture" (*Systematic Theology*, Augustus H. Strong, Judson Press, Valley Forge, Pa.).

Note from the above statement that the gift of prophecy does not involve new revelation but a clearer understanding or amplification of already-given truth.

The *Pulpit Commentary*, in its explanation of Paul's injunction, "Despise not prophesying" (1 Thes. 5:20), quotes Calvin, "By prophesying I do not understand the gift of foretelling the future, but the science of interpreting Scriptures, so that a prophet is an interpreter of the will of God."

An editorial in *Christianity Today* tells how in Zurich, Switzerland, in the 16th century, it was customary for all ministers and ministerial students to meet five times every week for "prophesying" which meant exegetical and systematic expositions of the Bible.

Thus, prophesying has come to mean the proclamation of the written Word of God in the wisdom and power of the Holy Spirit. And with clarity. Prophecy is linked with "light that shineth in a dark place" (2 Peter 1:19).

The gift of prophecy makes the Word of God relevant to a particular situation in a current context. As prophets of old poured forth their warnings of coming invasion because of national declension, so we need prophets today to inveigh against decadence in national life: racism, materialism, immorality, scientism, and a host of others, lest we suffer the decline and fall of our nations. Prophets are God's loudspeakers. How they are needed in national and local politics, education, journalism, family life, sports, and science! Prophecy applies the perennial Scripture to the present scene.

When we boil it down, prophecy ultimately has to do with Jesus Christ. Old Testament prophets foretold the coming of Christ. New Testament prophets centered their messages in the crucified, risen, and coming-again Lord Jesus. John wrote in a late chapter of the Bible, "The testimony of Jesus is the spirit of prophecy" (Rev. 19:10). All Scripture points to Christ. He is the sum and substance of the Old and New Testaments. Prophecy is Spirit-empowered proclamation of the Living Word who is the center and circumference of the written Word.

The result of exercise of the prophetic gift will be encouragement, edification, and comfort (1 Cor. 14:3). Not only are the comfortable to be disturbed, but the disturbed are to be comforted.

We might define the gift of prophecy as the Spirit-given ability to proclaim the written Word of God with clarity and to apply it to a particular situation with a view to correction or edification.

How Widespread is the Gift of Prophecy?

Prophecy ranks high among the gifts. In both the list of ministries (Eph. 4:11) and the list of gifts (1 Cor. 12:28), prophecy is given second spot, coming after the apostles in both instances. After the apostles founded the churches, the gift of prophecy was vital in the continued edification and correction of the church. Thus, it is not surprising to find apostles and prophets linked (Eph. 2:20).

Prophecy is specifically declared to be a superior gift. Because this vital gift of prophecy was often despised at Corinth while the inferior though more flamoyant gift of tongues was preferred, Paul devoted a long section to affirming the supremacy of prophecy over tongues (1 Cor. 14:1-25). If making the Word of God intelligible is necessary, tongues do not help but hinder. In giving an uncertain sound, they only erect a language barrier.

If this gift ranks so important, would we not expect it to be prevalent? Peter exercised the gift (along with the gift of evangelism) at Pentecost. Paul and his team used this Spirit-given ability on their missionary tours. Paul said that God "manifested His Word through *preaching*, which is committed unto me" (Titus 1:3). The Early Church had many prophets, who usually employed their gift in their own local congregation. Some eminent prophets itinerated. The *Didache* commanded that wandering prophets be supported, "Every true prophet who shall settle among you is worthy of his support." Each congregation had to exercise the gift of discernment to sift the true from the false.

Down through the centuries men have exercised the gift of prophecy—speaking forth for God. Some apply the title of prophet only to the eminent of church history. But Dr. Donald Grey Barnhouse widens its scope. "I do not agree with commentators who apply this test only to the giants of church history. God does not mean primarily Paul, Augustine, Luther, Calvin, Wesley, and so on. He is talking here about the little preacher up the north fork of Peak Creek; He is talking about those whom we call 'laymen,' although they form the vast majority of the body of Christ. This test really speaks to you and me" (*Commentary on the Epistle to the Romans*, Booklet No. 69, The Evangelical Foundation, Inc., Philadelphia, Pa.).

Theologian Frederick Dale Bruner would extend the significance of the gift beyond formal preaching, whether by clergymen or laymen, to informal interchange of uplifting conversation and advice. He says, "Paul sees the highest expression of spiritual gifts in the free, helpful discussion of Christians together and their contribution in thoughtful speech to each other. (It is, in fact, our impression that expressions such as 'thoughtful speech,' 'testimony,' or even 'counsel' better translate the word rendered now somewhat archaically 'prophecy.')" (*The Theology of the Holy Spirit*, Eerdmans, Grand Rapids, Mich.).

Conceivably the gift may extend to insight into and application of the Word to fellow believers' difficult situations, though this aspect shades somewhat into the gift of the word of wisdom.

Many agree that prophecy is not necessarily a formal discourse. Says Alexander Hay, "The modern distinction between the humble talk, or message, and the aristocratic sermon has no place in Scripture . . . There are, however, many varieties of the gift. The variety possessed by one may be the telling forth (preaching) of God's Word to adults; that of another may be for witness to children, or in the open air, or to unbelievers, or to believers, or to a small company of two or three, or to individuals. All are exercising the same gift for the . . . telling forth of the Gospel."

The gift may extend to proclamation over radio or TV, or in neighborhood Bible classes or small groups. Women in the Early Church possessed the gift (1 Cor. 11:5; Acts 21:8, 9). Says Hay, "This seems to be the gift most widely distributed. All believers are counseled to seek it (1 Cor. 14:1)." Then he adds, "Therefore all should possess it in one form or another" (*The New Testament Order for Church and Missionary*, cited earlier).

This opinion may be somewhat strong since Paul seems to teach that no gift is possessed by all. But certainly, if not all have it, many do—perhaps even most. Even if we have not the gift, we are enjoined to obey in this area.

Those who have the gift are to exercise it "according to the proportion of faith" (Rom. 12:6). Some take this to mean—employ your gift according to the canon of the objective faith once for all delivered to the saints. This interpretation would fit the emphasis that prophecy is no new inspiration adding to the sacred canon, but rather a new elucidation or amplification of truth already in the canon.

A second interpretation of proclaiming truth "according to the proportion of faith" is—speak forth the truth in the measure in which you have laid hold on the truth, or to the degree to which it is precious to you, or to the limit of your vision of that truth.

A third interpretation equates faith with gift, urging people to prophesy according to the measure of the gift. Whichever interpretation is correct, all express truth. Those with the gift must prophesy. And we must prophesy according to the objective propositional truth of the Word of God—and in the measure with which that truth has become meaningful to us. Let us prophesy!

One of the finest collections of rare and valuable violins belongs to a retired farmer in a small Saskatchewan prairie town. Among the 25 violins are some made by famous men like Stradivari. Since they have been collected as a hobby, they will not likely get much use. What melody could be heard were these instruments put in the hands of 25 talented violinists! Some churches contain collections of gifted Christians, many of whom have enhanced their potential with formal Bible school or college training. But no music is produced for the Master. Their gifts have become museum pieces—on display but not in use. The Lord needs gifted instruments.

Will you say with the Apostle Paul, "Woe is me if I preach (prophesy) not the Gospel"?

6

The Gift of Evangelism

Newsweek recently devoted its *Religion* page to a discussion of today's new-style evangelists. It pointed out that a whole new generation of young headliners is emerging. Tents are disappearing in favor of mass media. Concerts featuring ear-paralyzing Gospel rock, large-scale open-air baptismal services, crusades headlining sports and entertainment celebrities, all typify new-era evangelism.

Evangelists of the past have also often combined show and business techniques, according to this same *Newsweek* article. Eighteenth century revivals provided the theater for New England's working class. On the western frontier a century later, the local camp meeting was the best or only show in town.

If to the outsider evangelism smacks of show business, to the insider it has come to mean many different, often opposite, things. To some, evangelism in the Sunday evening service always ended with an invitation and all verses of "Just as I Am" sung through three times. Or evangelism is a two-week series of protracted services with an enthusiastic song leader and a flashy speaker (often an ex-addict or ex-pugilist or ex-entertainer or ex-convict), plus sawdust trail, mourners' bench, inquirers' room, and scalding tears.

To others, evangelism means something much more sedate, such as a confirmation or communicants' class, the giving of a cup of cold water, a silent witness to change the world, or even something so daring as the reciting of four steps of salvation.

Just what is the gift of evangelism?

The word *evangelism* does not occur in the Bible. In fact, it does not appear in the English language until the 17th century. The word *evangelist* occurs just three times in the New Testament, as follows:

Concerning Paul's trip back to Jerusalem, Luke writes, "And we entered into the house of Philip the evangelist, which was one of the seven; and abode with him" (Acts 21:8).

Speaking of the gifts of the ascended Christ, Paul writes, "And He gave some . . . evangelists" (Eph. 4:11).

In his last recorded letter, Paul urges Timothy to "do the work of an evangelist" (2 Tim. 4:5).

What Is the Gift of Evangelism?

Though all believers are to witness, the gift of evangelism is a special ability in communicating the Gospel message in relevant terms to unbelievers.

Unlike the missionary gift, the evangelistic gift does not involve witness across cultural lines.

Unlike the prophetic gift, it does not thunder judgment to the current scene but majors more in the grace of God.

Here's our definition—the gift of *proclaiming* the *Good News* of salvation *effectively* so that people respond to the claims of Christ in conversion and in *discipleship*.

Let's examine the four italicized terms in this definition.

1. Proclamation

In some circles today evangelism is spoken of as the "Christian presence." Almost total emphasis is placed on living a consistently godly life in one's environment. But the gift of evangelism is more than non-verbal influence. After all, Communists may heal, feed, and help, but this social presence isn't Gospel preaching. The gift of evangelism requires words in addition to works.

At some time explanation will have to be given as to how a sinner can become rightly related to God. Announcement of the Good News of Christ's historical, redemptive death and resurrection will have to be made verbally. Evangelism is one of the "speaking" gifts. No one is saved by observing a quiet, godly life, though such certainly prepares the soil for the seed of God's Word.

Missionary statesman Samuel H. Moffett tells of a work in Taegu, Korea, which has two medical missionary doctors, but 120 qualified Korean medical doctors, every one of whom is a Christian and belongs to the hospital's Preaching Society. These doctors minister to human needs with their medical expertise. But because evangelism demands speaking about Jesus Christ, teams of doctors and nurses circulate weekends to rural areas where medical help is unavailable to give free daytime care to the sick and to conduct evening evangelistic services. As a result of this biblical combination of healing and heralding, more than a hundred new churches have sprung up in the Taegu area.

Evangelism is not just presence; it is proclamation.

2. Good News

That which is proclaimed has intellectual content. The word *gospel* comes from two Greek words, *well* and *announcement*. Thus the Gospel is good *announcement* or *Good News*. The gift of evangelism involves proclaiming the Good News.

But what good news? It is the thrilling report of something that happened historically which can bring unsearchable riches presently. Because the Lord Jesus Christ, very God and very man, died for my sins on the cross over 19 centuries ago, was buried and rose the third day, God the Father can accept His Son's sacrifice as full satisfaction for my guilt. If I reach forth by faith to receive Christ as my personal Saviour, I am declared righteous by God, not through any merit of mine but through the merits of Christ's shed blood. No longer exposed to the penalty of the broken Law, I am bestowed with full sonship in the divine family. As I come to understand more of the Gospel's implications, I rejoice in pardon for the past, strength for the present (through the ministry of the regenerating and indwelling Spirit), and a living hope for the future. This is indeed Good News.

Biblical evangelism will appeal to the intellect as well as to the emotions. The abbreviated accounts of sermons in Acts should not misguide us into supposing that the apostles made naive and hasty appeals for decisions without challenging man's powers of thought. Paul could lecture, discuss, and dialogue for hours on end, day after day, even spending two or three years in some places. He testified strenuously, proclaimed forcefully, refuted thoroughly, reasoned closely.

The Sanhedrin accused the apostles, "You have filled Jerusalem with your teaching," which could not have been said unless their evangelism proclaimed a body of truth. Michael Green in *Evangelism in the Early Church* says, "The fashionable separation . . .

of . . . kerygma from didache, preaching from teaching, in primitive evangelism is misleading, and unconsciously perhaps supports this suspicion that the Apostles appealed primarily to the emotions. In fact, evangelism is called teaching in several places in Acts. The hearers would inevitably want to know a good deal about Jesus before putting their faith in Him" (Eerdmans, Grand Rapids, Mich.).

Though the evangelistic gift should be distinguished from the teaching gift, true evangelism must embody some teaching. Without sufficient intellectual foundation, the Early Church would not have lasted long. As in every age, people made a commitment of faith based on evidence, not a leap in the dark. The hearer's emotions may or may not be moved, but his reason must not be bypassed.

Because of the essentiality of doctrinal content in solid evangelism, one history professor claims that John Calvin (along with Martin Luther and John Wesley) "stands out as one of the most successful evangelists in modern church history. Calvin was not simply to convert the city of Geneva or even the cantons of French-speaking Switzerland; he was to become an 'evangelist of Europe,' spreading the evangelical faith from Scotland to Transylvania. This achievement came through his skillful synthesis of theology and evangelism. Calvin is an excellent example of the theologian as an evangelist" ("John Calvin: Theologian and Evangelist," C. George Fry, Copyright 1970 by Christianity Today).

Though we may find it difficult to think of that theological classic, Calvin's Institutes, as an evangelistic appeal, he stated in his preface that his intention was "to give instruction to those who long to be children of God, primarily among my fellow countrymen. For I saw many in France hunger and thirst after Christ, yet few who receive true instruction about Him" (as cited above). It's not surprising to learn that "in less than 11 years, from 1555 to 1566, 121 evangelists, personally trained by Calvin, were dispatched into persecuted France from Geneva. In their first four years those pioneer Presbyterian evangelists founded 2,000 new French Calvinist congregations" ("What is Evangelism?" Samuel H. Moffett, Copyright 1969 by Christianity Today).

Thus, the exercise of the evangelistic gift will promote a doctrinal content. Church historians tell us that, through the centuries, theological advances have preceded evangelistic surges. If we are going to proclaim something, we must have something to proclaim. The urgency and thrill of a message motivates its spread. Without real content evangelism fizzles.

3. Effectively—resulting in conversion

The gift of evangelism, moreover, involves the proclamation of the Good News effectively so that people respond to the claims of Christ.

Not that there is a response every time we witness. Campus Crusade for Christ defines success in witnessing as "sharing Christ in the power of the Spirit and leaving the results to Him." However, when the evangelistic gift is present, faithful witnessing will from time to time yield affirmative responses.

When Peter preached at Pentecost, his hearers "were pricked in their heart, and said . . . Men and brethren, what shall we do?" (Acts 2:37) The result was conversion and baptism of 3,000.

On their missionary journey that took them to Iconium, Paul and Barnabas went into the synagogue and "so spake that a great multitude both of the Jews and also of the Greeks believed" (Acts 14:1).

Repeatedly through Acts, after proclamation of the Good News, people believed. The gift communicates the Gospel with power so that people are brought into the experience of salvation. The gift of evangelism has been defined as the ability to present the Good News with clarity, poise, and some degree of success. Perhaps the gentle wooing of people across the line of decision into the fold of Christ is part of this gift.

Even when an affirmative decision is not registered, the gift of evangelism so effectively confronts people with the claims of Christ that they have to decide eventually for or against. After Paul spoke boldly in the synagogue at Ephesus for three months, his listeners were forced to a yes or no. Tragically, many "were hardened, and believed not, but spake evil of that way before the multitude" (Acts 19:9). After Paul's reasoning of righteousness, temperance, and judgment to come, Governor Felix tremblingly rejected the faith (Acts 24:25).

The evangelistic gift renders the Gospel proclamation a savor of life unto life, or of death unto death.

4. Discipleship

Real evangelistic ability doesn't stop at conversion, but desires to see the convert in continuous growth in the fellowship of the church. If no church exists in the area, an evangelist may organize a church to nurture new believers. Some Bible scholars include church-planting under the gift of evangelism when done within one's culture. To church-plant cross-culturally requires the missionary gift.

Where churches do exist, the evangelist will not need to initiate any new work but will feed the converts into these fellowships. Dedicated evangelists and evangelical organizations have aggressive and systematic follow-up procedures for new converts. Billy Graham has long shown such concern. Lest those making profession be left to sink or swim, his organization provides courses to encourage Christlikeness. Campus Crusade has perfected the *Way of Life* plan for a church to guide new converts in understanding the faith, growing in grace, and launching out in witness.

Who Has the Gift of Evangelism?

Reams have been written on evangelism. Essays could be multiplied on various phases: motivation, meeting excuses, qualifications, neglect, securing prospects, methods, need to be winsome if we would win some, pointers such as "It's hard to convince a person you wish him in the heavenly home if you don't want him in your earthly home."

Our concern has been to define the nature of the gift, and now to examine its distribution. How widespread is this gift?

No one could doubt that D. L. Moody, Percy Crawford of Pinebrook and The King's College, Jack Wyrtzen of Word of Life, Bill Bright of Campus Crusade, and Billy Graham possess or possessed the gift of evangelism. But how many believers in the average congregation have it? Do you have it?

Campus Crusade estimates it takes 1,000 laymen and six pastors one year to win one convert to Christ. Surely, since the Lord wishes the Gospel proclaimed effectively to every last person in our culture, to say nothing of all the cultures of the world, He must have given the gift of evangelism to large numbers of believers. At least to enough Christians so it wouldn't take a thousand of them to win one soul a year!

The gift is not restricted to the pastor or the professional. Philip, the only person called an evangelist in the Bible, was a deacon. A Bible conference speaker asked a young man at the end of a service if he had ever won a soul to Christ. Answering no, the youth added, "That's the preacher's job."

The speaker countered, "Didn't you ever read how the early Christians who were scattered abroad went everywhere preaching the Word?"

"But those were the apostles," the young man replied.

"I beg your pardon," responded the speaker. "Will you please read Acts 8, beginning at the first verse?"

The youth read, "And at that time there was a great persecution against the church which was at Jerusalem; and they were scattered abroad throughout the regions of Judea and Samaria, except the apostles."

The surprised young man learned that those who went everywhere evangelizing were specifically not the apostles, but so-called laymen. The Early Church was a lay movement. Though all the apostles doubtless possessed the gift of evangelism, so did multitudes of the early saints. It's likely that in all ages, including ours, far more believers have this gift than are aware of it.

Church programs and city-wide evangelism do reach masses of people, but they also miss multitudes—ghetto dwellers, hippies, high-rise apartment tenants, folks on relief, artists, college students, and hosts of other unchurched people. Just as fishermen do not fish in an aquarium they have stocked with fish, soul-winners will not find the sacred enclosure of a church building the best place to exercise their witness. The Early Church evangelized in the open air, on highways, in houses, by rivers, in jails, in the intellectual arena as at Mars Hill, at court. "In the history of the church more people have been won to Christ by such quiet ways than in great mass meetings" ("What is Evangelism?" cited previously, page 59). Through rubbing shoulders with the unevangelized, the person in the pew, more than the preacher in the pulpit, has opportunity for witness in the workaday world. Is it not logical to believe, therefore, that the Spirit has given the gift of evangelism to large numbers of laymen?

A full chapter (Acts 8) devoted to the labors of Philip the evangelist recounts both his city-wide campaign in Samaria and his desert trip to reach a lone Ethiopian traveler on the Gaza highway. Not wishing to chain Christ to the pulpit of a church, many saints through the centuries have been led, as Philip was, out into the highways and byways to carry a witness. C. T. Studd,

famed missionary to three continents, wrote:
"Some want to live within the sound
Of church or chapel bell;
I want to run a rescue ship
Within a yard of hell."
Many are the attempts to reach the unchurched in our day.
May not the proliferation of current innovative ministries and
methods with an evangelistic thrust, as listed below, indicate that
the gift of evangelism is widely present?

Agriculture	Hospital visitation
Beach	Institutional
Bible distribution	Jewish
Breakfasts	Letter-writing
Businessmen's luncheons	Literature
Camps	Magic
Child evangelism	Music festivals
Coffeehouses	Newspapers
College campus	Open air
Cults	Phone
Door-to-door calling	Prison
Drug rehabilitation	Radio
Films	Rescue missions
Foreign students	Servicemen's centers
Friendship	Sports
High school groups	TV
Home Bible studies	Tracts
	Visitation

Even so, only a fraction of professing Christians today actively
engage in any of the above list. Since witnessing is a top priority
in the hierarchy of duties for the child of God, should not flocks
of believers be active in some form of sharing the Good News? If
Christians were faithful in discharging their duty in witnessing,
many would discover that they have the gift of evangelism which
has lain dormant since their regeneration by the Holy Spirit.

Why haven't more believers discovered they possess this gift?
Simply and mainly because they have not exposed themselves to
what John Calvin called the "most urgent work of the Christian
church"—personal evangelism.

If we can talk about the Detroit Tigers, the Miami Dolphins,
the Montreal Canadiens, the New York Knickerbockers, politics,

weather, and our cars, surely we can talk about Jesus Christ. Many a person has been helped to overcome his timidity, ignorance, and lack of confidence through attendance at a Campus Crusade Lay Institute for Evangelism where he has learned the basics of the abundant life and the know-how to lead a person to Christ. Then going out with fear and trepidation on a house-to-house survey, he has discovered after timidly knocking on some doors and nervously stammering through the Four Spiritual Laws that the Holy Spirit has blessed his stumbling witness. Encouraged, he has gone on to a sense of at-homeness and deep-down delight, and has had some success in sharing his faith. He has awakened to the existence of the gift of evangelism.

One pastor who made a special study of charismata estimated that half the active membership of any evangelical church might possess this gift.

Do you know that the great evangelist D. L. Moody wasn't always interested in winning people to Christ? At first his main passion was in getting people to attend Sunday School. He relates how he began to discover his gift of evangelism.

"When I went to Chicago, I hired four pews in a church and used to go out on the street and pick up young men and fill these pews. I never spoke to the young men about their souls; that was the work of elders, I thought. After working for some time like that, I started a mission Sunday School. I thought numbers were everything, and so I worked for numbers. When the attendance ran below 1,000 it troubled me, and when it ran to 1,200 or 1,500 I was elated. Still none were converted; there was no harvest. Then God opened my eyes."

One Sunday Moody filled in for an ill teacher of a class of young ladies. They were so frivolous that Moody felt like telling them never to return. The teacher, learning he was seriously ill, confided in Moody, "I've never led any of my class to Christ. I really believe I've done the girls more harm than good."

Says Moody, "I had never heard anyone talk like that before, and it set me thinking."

Later Moody said to the teacher, "Suppose you go and tell them how you feel. I'll go with you in a carriage, if you want to go."

The teacher consented. Says Moody, "We started out together. It was one of the best journeys I ever had on earth." He tells how they would go to the house of one of the girls, and the teacher would talk to her about her soul. No frivolity then, rather tears. After the teacher explained the way of life, he suggested Moody pray. Moody had never done such a thing in his life as to pray to God to convert a young lady there and then. But he prayed. God answered. They went to other houses. The teacher would go upstairs, be all out of breath, then tell the girls why he had come. Before long they would break down and seek salvation.

When the teacher's strength would wane, Moody would take him home for the night. Next evening they would go out again. At the end of 10 days his face was shining. "Mr. Moody, the last one of my class has yielded herself to Christ."

Because the teacher was moving from the area, Moody called the class together for a prayer meeting. The dying teacher sat in the midst and read John 14. They tried to sing, "Blest be the tie that binds." Then they knelt to pray. Every member of the class prayed for her teacher. Says Moody, "That night God kindled a fire in my soul that has never gone out. The height of my ambition had been to be a successful merchant." Unlike the rich young ruler, he turned his back on money. From then on, soul-winning was his business. Discovering his gift he employed it to his dying day. (*The Life of Dwight L. Moody,* W. R. Moody, Fleming Revell.)

Even if we do not have the gift of evangelism, we are to do the work of an evangelist. Jesus said, "Come ye after me, and I will make you to become fishers of men" (Mark 1:17). As we launch out into the deep, perhaps we will discover that we have a Spirit-implanted ability—the gift of evangelism.

7

The Gift
of Shepherding

An increasingly popular method of building Sunday School attendance is the bus ministry. Visitors from a church canvass trailercourts, new developments, apartment complexes, military establishments, or go door-to-door in established localities, to find boys and girls whose parents will permit them to ride a church bus to and from Sunday School. Some churches have as many as 70 or 80 buses picking up hundreds of children every week from all over town.

A book explaining the mechanics of this ministry devotes one section to the bus captain, who according to the author is virtually a bus pastor. He is required to visit the homes of those who ride regularly, is constantly available to the families for any needs they might have. Like a shepherd seeking lost sheep, he is to seek out wandering and delinquent riders. He is responsible for showing genuine interest in those in the hospital, in families where deaths have occurred, and in situations of serious financial need. He must also maintain discipline on the bus to and from Sunday School. In essence, he is a pastor to his riders, even though not a pastor in the formal sense.

You Don't Have to Be a Pastor to Have the Gift of Pastoring

The word *pastor* occurs numerous times in the Old Testament, especially in Jeremiah where it generally refers to civil leaders, kings, rulers, and magistrates, usually in terms of strong condemnation for negligence—for failure to feed the flock and for scattering the sheep without proper care (Jer. 2:8; 3:15; 10:21; 12:10; 23: 1-4).

The word *pastor* occurs only once in the New Testament. "And He gave some . . . pastors" (Eph. 4:11). Pastor refers to an office in the church, usually considered synonymous with that of bishop and elder. However, though everyone divinely called to the office of pastor will of necessity receive the corresponding gift of pastoring from the Holy Spirit, not every one who has the gift of pastoring has been called to the office of pastor. You may have the gift of pastoring without being a pastor.

Though the English word *pastor* occurs but once in the King James New Testament, the same Greek word occurs several times, is translated shepherd, and usually has reference to the Lord Jesus Christ. For example, the Apostle John speaks of the Good Shepherd knowing His sheep and giving His life for them (John 10:11, 14). The benediction in Hebrews invokes "our Lord Jesus Christ, that great Shepherd of the sheep" (13:20). Peter tells his readers, "For ye were as sheep going astray; but are now returned unto the Shepherd and Bishop of your souls" (1 Peter 2:25). Later in the same epistle, Peter exhorts the elders to feed their flocks so that "when the Chief Shepherd shall appear, ye shall receive a crown of glory that fadeth not away" (5:4). The title of Chief Shepherd strongly infers the existence of under-shepherds. Many a believer who has not been called to the office of pastor has been given this shepherding gift.

A little flower girl at a wedding rehearsal was introduced to the minister. She asked him, "Are you a pastor or a preacher?"

Taken back by the question, the minister asked, "Do you know the difference?"

She thought a moment, then answered, "A preacher thinks more of himself, but a pastor thinks more of his people."

Whether or not some preachers concentrate too much on themselves, a true pastor does devote himself to the flock. The characteristics of the pastoral gift can be illustrated in the life of the ancient shepherd.

Nature of the Shepherding Gift
1. To Guide
The word *pastor* conjures up the pastoral scene of Psalm 23—a shepherd gently leading his flock beside still waters and making

them to lie down in green pastures. Portraying the coming Messiah-Shepherd, the prophet wrote, "He shall gather the lambs with His arms, and carry them in His bosom, and shall gently lead those that are with young" (Isa. 40:11).

Both staff and rod helped to guide. When a lamb entangled its foot in the underbrush, the shepherd hooked the staff around the lamb's leg to tenderly ease it out of its prison of thorns.

Though the rod was used on the enemy, it also served another purpose. Sometimes long stretches of overgrown briars, thistles, and weeds stood in the way. To go all the way around would mean quite a detour. To go through would mean tearing and scratching the animals. So, the shepherd would take the rod, swing it from side to side, and move slowly forward. Beating down the thorns, he would make a path through the infested patch for the sheep to follow unhurt.

When the shepherd saw mountainous terrain ahead, involving a long, steep climb along a narrow and dangerous path, he often made the sheep first lie down in green fields. This helped remove the risk of overtiredness and the danger of resultant fall over the precipice. Quietness and rest provided renewal of strength for strenuous travel.

Susie, a fairly new Christian and a high school senior, had been swept off her feet in a whirlwind courtship by a fine Christian who was a college junior. After only three weeks of acquaintance, they announced, quietly among youthful friends, not only their informal engagement but also their intent to get married in about two months' time.

Here was definite need for someone with the shepherding gift, perhaps a Sunday School teacher, youth advisor, or fellow student, to gently guide her in paths of righteous sanity. Providentially, a former youth leader whom Susie respected greatly pointed out that neither had a job, that far too insufficient time had elapsed for them to begin to know each other, that the Bible presents a serious view of marriage which demands much more consideration before entering that high and holy estate, especially for teenagers. Not the pastor, but a former youth leader with the Spirit-empowered pastoral gift, shepherded her from her rash and precipitous course.

2. To Graze

The major duty of the shepherd was to lead the sheep into fields for grazing. Old Testament pastors were to "feed you with knowledge and understanding" (Jer. 3:15). The coming Messiah "shall feed His flock like a shepherd" (Isa. 40:11).

Three times in the New Testament the verb form of *pastor* is used, each time with the meaning of providing food. First, Jesus, when recommissioning repentant Peter, said, "Feed My sheep" (John 21:16). Second, Paul exhorted the Ephesian elders "to feed the church of God" (Acts 20:28). Third, Peter addressed the elders to "feed the flock of God which is among you" (1 Peter 5:2). Etymologically, *pastor* comes from the verb "to feed." Literally, the pastor was the "feeder of the sheep."

A student of Palestinian culture says that the shepherd directed his flock into the best of pastures. On the journey he would note on some high bank, perhaps beyond reach of the sheep, luscious and juicy herbs, which he would pluck. Also, high on trees might be tasty morsels. So up would go his staff, down would come a branch, and off would fall these tidbits.

Similarly, the pastor of a spiritual flock must feed his followers the Word of God. Pastor and teacher are associated in the list of offices by Paul. In fact, some scholars link them in one office: "pastor-teacher" (see Eph. 4:11).

But the feeding gift is not confined to the pastorate. Mr. and Mrs. Jones, who had just accepted Christ in an evangelistic crusade, stood in dire need of nurture. Their neighbors, some years older in the faith, invited the Joneses to their home for an evening, engaged them in some Bible study, and were able to open up the biblical basics to the new converts. They also directed them to the Sunday School class dealing with "Growing in the Christian Life." Before long they introduced them into a neighborhood couples' Bible study. Exercising their shepherding gift, these neighbors have not only fed Mr. and Mrs. Jones, but have steered them into other pastures where they will likewise receive spiritual nourishment.

3. To Guard

The shepherd protected from hostile influences. When young David volunteered to fight Goliath, King Saul doubted that a youth could match skill with a long-time man of war like the giant. But David replied, "Thy servant kept his father's sheep, and there came a lion, and a bear, and took a lamb out of the flock; and I went out after him, and smote him, and delivered it out of his mouth; and when he arose against me, I caught him by his beard,

and smote him, and slew him. Thy servant slew both the lion and
the bear . . . The Lord that delivered me out of the paw of the
lion, and out of the paw of the bear, He will deliver me out of
the hand of this Philistine (1 Sam. 17:34-37).

To keep wild animals at a distance, the shepherd carried a
sling, which he learned to use with great skill. Such a sling David
used to fell Goliath.

The shepherd also used the sling for another purpose. When a
sheep, roaming at some distance suddenly fell into danger, the
shepherd could fling a stone with such accuracy that, landing
just beyond the animal, it would alarm the sheep into turning
back for protection.

If the enemy approached too closely, or attacked, the shepherd
used his rod. Doubtless David used the club-like weapon to slay
the lion and bear.

To prevent the sheep from suffering sunstroke, the shepherd
would anoint their heads with oil. Camels have been known to
collapse in the desert sun and die, because they had not been
rubbed with oil.

Though a hireling would flee in time of danger, a genuine
shepherd would protect his flock to the utmost, even laying down
his life if necessary. Well known is Jesus' parable of the shepherd
seeking the lone, lost sheep.

Paul knew that false teachers would dog his steps, hounding the
flocks he established. This is why he urged the Ephesian elders,
"Take heed therefore unto yourselves, and to all the flock over
which the Holy Ghost hath made you overseers, to feed the church
of God, which He hath purchased with His own blood. For I know
this, that after my departing shall grievous wolves enter in among
you, not sparing the flock. Also of your own selves shall men
arise, speaking perverse things, to draw away disciples after them.
Therefore watch" (Acts 20:28-31).

Mrs. X, a widow, had just made a profession of faith. Her progress was slow. One day a Christian friend was alarmed to learn
that Mrs. X had opened her home to a Jehovah's Witness for a
weekly Bible study. The friend, at first inclined to phone her
pastor for his help, instead visited Mrs. X and kindly but accurately outlined the basic errors of this cult. Mrs. X, becoming
aware of the Scriptural deviations, broke off the weekly Bible
study with the Jehovah's Witnesses, and continued to grow in the

truth. Her friend had exercised the pastoral gift.

For one pastor to keep an alert eye on hundreds of sheep lest they begin to wander is utterly impossible, nor was it ever meant to be. Thus the need for those with the shepherding gift in the church "able . . . to admonish one another" (Rom. 15:14). When any of the flock disobeyed the Lord's commands, it was the saints (not the pastor) who were to "admonish him as a brother" (2 Thes. 3:15).

Areas of Exercise Today

The position of dean of men (or women) at our colleges provides wide latitude for the use of the pastoral gift. How many youth, away from home and local church influence, need someone to turn to for guidance? Professors and mature believers in college towns also need to be sensitive to the plight of God's bewildered and sometimes wandering flock in their midst.

A young man joined a local evangelical church. A year later, his name and picture were splashed on the front page of the area newspaper for impersonating a police officer. One of his fellow church members, in the train of the Good Shepherd, spent the next Sunday afternoon tracing the delinquent down, praying with him, and then bringing him to the midweek prayer meeting, where the lawbreaker asked forgiveness of God and church.

Sunday School teachers and youth advisors have ample opportunity to utilize the shepherding gift. Young people characteristically turn to some older person other than their own parents for direction.

Older Christian women can shepherd younger wives in family problems and domestic situations. Paul exhorted the aged women to be "in behavior as becometh holiness . . . that they may teach the young women to be sober, to love their husbands, to love their children, to be discreet, chaste, keepers at home, good, obedient to their own husbands, that the Word of God be not blasphemed" (Titus 2:3-5).

Christian youth should be on the lookout for young people who are beginning to drift, or who seem to be floundering, but who can be drawn back to the fold by the gifted use of the shepherding staff.

Believers with this gift can maneuver some poorly fed lamb into a neighborhood Bible class or sound evangelical church. After a lady visited a Gospel-preaching church to hear a special speaker, a visitor from the church dropped by to express welcome. Learning the name of the lady's home church, the visitor cautiously expressed doubt as to whether that church preached the Gospel. Three years later the lady showed up again in church, sought out the lady who had visited her, confessed she had been angered when first told her home church did not preach the Bible, but now admitted that the charge was true. She came regularly, joined, became active. But a gentle word of warning had started this course of action.

Through the writing of letters and articles some express the gift of shepherding. Much content in Paul's letters guides, feeds, and guards. In fact, three of his letters (1 and 2 Timothy, Titus) are called "pastoral epistles," for they tell shepherds Timothy and Titus how to shepherd.

Some churches have a "shepherd plan" for new believers. Each new Christian is assigned a mature believer whose responsibility is to take the new convert under his wing, see that he attends services regularly, call him if absent, encourage him in daily reading of the Bible and prayer, guard him from false teaching, and guide him into some form of Christian service where his gifts can be used.

The office of the pastor was given to help mature the saints with a view to their Christian service. Not surprisingly, a major aspect of the non-official gift of shepherding is helping others to discover their gifts and then guiding them into channels of ministry.

Some men preeminently have this gift of shepherding believers into outlets of service. One man with major influence over the ministries of many well-known Christian leaders of this past generation was Paul Rader, one-time pastor of Moody Church, Chicago.

One day Rader challenged a new young convert to help with junior boys.

The young man replied, "But I'm in engineering and work some Sundays."

Rader retorted, "Why don't you quit that job? You pray about it and I'll pray too."

Within a week the young man was offered the position of manager of the Tabernacle Publishing Company. The jump from engineering to publishing started a series of events which ultimately led to the establishment of a large and influential Christian publishing house. The young man and his wife were Drs. Victor and Bernice Cory, founders of Scripture Press.

Others influenced in their Christian ministry through the shepherding gift of Rader were Dr. V. R. Edman, who became president of Wheaton College; Dr. Howard Ferrin, who presided over Providence Bible Institute and later became Chancellor of Barrington College; and Merrill Dunlap, well-known Gospel song composer, to name just a few.

Perhaps more Christians than realize it possess the shepherding gift. If more Christians would guide, feed, and guard fellow-believers, not so much counseling would have to be done by the church staff. This would not only eliminate much wear and tear on the official pastor, but also it would meet many needs that otherwise might go unmet.

8

The Gift of Teaching

The third largest fleet in the world is the famed "mothball" navy, comprised of 768 ships anchored in various U.S. harbors. In emergency these vessels could be readied for action in less than three months. To preserve them, each has been repainted and treated with a protective coating. All openings have been blocked. Steel and aluminum "igloos" have been built over exposed equipment. Inside the various compartments, dehumidifiers hum on. Outside, rust and corrosion are combated by electrodes ringing the hulls with a continuous electric current, which blocks the normal chemical reaction.

Sad to say, many believers seem to be in mothballs. Anchored in some sheltered ecclesiastical harbor, they forget that spiritual war rages. The church should not be inactively isolated up some religious river, but should be on the high seas fighting the foe.

One gift many Christians seem to have put in mothballs is that of teaching. With so many Sunday Schools and other spots of service crying for competent Spirit-filled teachers, or complaining because of pedagogical misfits, every believer should examine his own life to see whether he possesses this gift. If he does, he should be using it. If he doesn't, he should quit trying.

The gift of teaching is the *supernatural ability* to *explain clearly* and *apply effectively* the *truth of the Word* of God. The definition contains four concepts to be amplified in this chapter: supernatural ability, clear communication, effective application, and body of truth.

Supernatural Ability

Though every gift requires supernatural ability, the point is stressed here because of the inevitable question, "If a person is capable of teaching, will he automatically have the gift of teaching on becoming a Christian?" The answer is, not automatically; only if the Spirit chooses to give this gift. But it is more likely than not that the Spirit will bestow the gift of teaching on one who already has the talent. The Spirit of God, who operates decently and in order, would likely build His gift with supernatural power upon the foundation of the talent already there. But not always.

Strong similarities exist between the talent and the gift. Both deal with communication of truth. But as charted below, vital differences exist:

Talent	*Gift*
Present from natural birth	Present from spiritual birth
Operates through common grace in society	Operates through special grace and the church
Communicates any subject	Communicates biblical truth
Often yields just understanding of topic	Prepares for involvement and obedience

All the courses given in graduate educational schools to sharpen pedagogical skill can never spark the divine plus that makes the difference between natural talent and supernatural gift. On the other hand, a person without formal education can become a Spirit-gifted teacher of spiritual truth.

In his book *Body Life,* Dr. Ray C. Stedman sums it up, "It is quite possible, therefore, for a Christian to have a talent for teaching, but not to have the spiritual gift of teaching. If that is the case and he were asked to teach a Sunday School class, as an example, he would be quite capable of imparting considerable information and knowledge of facts about the lessons to his class but his teaching would lack the power to bless, to advance his students spiritually. This fact helps to explain the many qualified secular teachers who do not do well at all as Sunday School teachers. On the other hand, many school teachers also possess, as Christians, the spiritual gift of teaching and are greatly used of God in Bible classes and Sunday School teaching."

Clear Communication

1. Master Teacher

Reams have been written on the pedagogical principles used

by Jesus. He is still the ideal model for today. He began where people were, using at-hand, simple things like sheep, vines, candles, to go on to the new and unfamiliar. Often He asked questions; over 100 times, someone has counted. He frequently countered a question with a question. He illustrated by parables. He took advantage of occasions to make a point. At a dinner He spoke of people who made excuses for not coming to God's great banquet. He taught by example, as when He washed the disciples' feet.

Possession of the gift of teaching does not guarantee polished ability to communicate truth. The gift needs to be developed. Hence, the gifted teacher shows no inconsistency nor lack of faith by studying Jesus' teaching methods, taking courses in pedagogy, and using helps such as flannelgraph, overhead projector, films, cassettes, or charts.

2. *Association with prophetic gift*

Clear communication of truth is involved in many speaking gifts. The missionary who transplants the Gospel across cultural lines, the evangelist who proclaims the Good News, the shepherd who feeds his sheep the Word of life, all have in common the clear explanation of truth. But the gift most frequently linked with that of teaching is the prophetic.

Prophecy and pedagogy are the only two gifts mentioned in every one of Paul's three lists.

The two gifts are mentioned together in Acts 5:42: "And daily in the Temple, and in every house, they ceased not to teach and preach Jesus Christ."

In the church at Antioch were "certain prophets and teachers" (Acts 13:1). Two of them, Paul and Barnabas, continued "teaching and preaching the Word of the Lord" (Acts 15:35).

Perhaps one reason Paul gathered a team of helpers around him was to balance the prophesying and the teaching. Some may have been more gifted at announcing or proclaiming truth (prophesying or preaching) while others excelled at explaining (teaching) it. Some pounded it home; others expounded it. Paul combined both gifts. When he dwelt two years as a prisoner in his own hired house at Rome, he received all who came to him, "preaching the kingdom of God, and teaching those things which concern the Lord Jesus Christ" (Acts 28:30, 31).

Prophecy and pedagogical gifts were also associated in the ministry of Christ. "Jesus went about all Galilee, teaching in their synagogues, and preaching the Gospel of the kingdom" (Matt. 4:23). But far more is said of His teaching than His preaching. He was the Master Teacher.

Effective Application

The gift of teaching should involve more than impartation of information; it should lead to involvement of the individual. Dr. Lawrence O. Richards in *Creative Bible Teaching* identifies five levels in the process of learning. Unless the fifth step is reached, true teaching has not taken place.

First is the rote level, which elicits a response from memory, perhaps meaningless to the learner.

Second is the recognition level, at which a pupil can recognize something that was said in class, as to whether true or false.

Third is the restatement level, when the student grasps the idea sufficiently to restate it in his own words.

Fourth is the relational level, when the student discovers a personal meaning.

Fifth is the realizational level, when the student makes the fact real in experience, not only understanding what response is required but making that response in deed.

Two little brothers, both in the Beginner Department but in separate classes, had studied the same lesson one morning. It dealt with the miracle of Jesus feeding the 5,000 with a lunch shared by a small boy. On the way home, each could tell his parents the story with accurate detail. But five minutes after arrival home, they were engaged in violent argument because they wouldn't share a toy. They hadn't really learned.

A senior high class studying 2 Corinthians came across the verse, "Be ye not unequally yoked together with unbelievers" (6:14). Susie, who had been dating a non-Christian boy quite steadily, grasped the truth on the first three levels. She was able to express in her own words that Christians should not be intimately associated with non-Christians. When its personal meaning dawned on her, she realized she would have to make a decision about her going steady with an unbeliever. The truth really got through to her when she decided to call her boyfriend that very afternoon and cool their relationship. The senior high teacher was enabled by the Spirit's gift of teaching to help her pupil relate to and realize the truth personally.

A visitor in a college class heard the story of Joseph's resistance to the repeated temptations by Potiphar's wife. He went out to reject the allurements of a married woman who had been deliberately crossing his path. The skillful presentation of a gifted teacher under the unction of the Holy Spirit had a decisive influence upon him.

Though it may be blocked by the obduracy of the stubborn heart, the gift of teaching should lead students to the practice of biblical precepts. Says Richards, "This kind of creativity is not something the church can afford to leave to the exceptional teacher. It's the heart of the ministry it expects from every teacher."

A Body of Truth

A 20-year-old street lad was won to Christ through a coffeehouse ministry. Six months later he was asked, "Who is Jesus?" He answered, "The greatest ever, the finest Man that ever lived." This limited, incomplete, humanistic answer pointed up the need for indoctrination.

In the face of the anti-intellectual trend of today, we need to remind ourselves of the truth content of Christianity. All new converts need to know that Christianity involves not only excitement but instruction. Enthusiasm apart from biblical teaching is contrary to the spirit of divine revelation. (Of course, truth without enthusiasm is also inconsistent with God's Word.) Zeal should be given direction by knowledge; and knowledge comes from the body of truth, the Bible. The now generation activists often prefer emotion over truth. Dr. John R. W. Stott says, "Experience without truth is the menace of a mindless Christianity."

Because Christianity cannot survive apart from a body of truth, teaching has been a vital, central, and indispensable part in the ongoing of the church. Jesus' Great Commission made teaching an integral part of the program of His followers. When people are evangelized (teaching is involved in communicating the Good News), and become disciples, they are to be baptized (once for all), and then taught (a continuing process to the end of their days). The final verse in Matthew says, "Teaching them to observe all things whatsoever I have commanded you" (28:20).

No wonder that immediately after the conversion of the 3,000 on the Day of Pentecost, "they continued steadfastly in the apostles' doctrine [teaching]" (Acts 2:42).

The Sanhedrin, grieved that the apostles taught the people, imprisoned Peter and John. They later released them with the command to "not speak at all nor *teach* in the name of Jesus" (4:18). But the apostles continued to teach. Again arrested, the apostles were awakened by an angel at night and told to speak in the Temple. The apostles "entered into the Temple early in the morning, and *taught*" (5:21). The bewildered Sanhedrin was told, "Behold, the men whom ye put in prison are standing in the Temple, and *teaching* the people (5:25). Even after they were beaten, the apostles "ceased not to *teach . . . Jesus* Christ" (5:42).

Barnabas and Paul *taught* new believers a whole year at Antioch (11:26). At Corinth, Paul continued "a year and six months, *teaching* the word of God among them" (18:11). The work of the Lord demanded continuous teaching of both new and established believers. At Ephesus, Paul *taught* "publicly and from house to house" for two years (19:10; 20:20). The charge brought against Paul which precipitated a two-hour uproar was, "This is the man that *teacheth* all men everywhere" (21:28).

Teaching is essential to the chain of communication. "The things that thou hast heard of me among many witnesses, the same commit thou to faithful men, who shall be able to teach others also" (2 Tim. 2:2). Four links can be discerned: Paul to Timothy to faithful men who will teach others. But it's the same content of truth that is taught from link to link. No wonder Paul commanded Timothy to give attention to teaching (1 Tim. 4:13, 16).

Significantly, the gift of teaching seems to be the main and perhaps the only required gift for a pastor of Christian worker. The *fruit* of the Spirit seems far more necessary than gifts. In the list of qualifications for bishop (elder, pastor) in 1 Timothy 3:1-7, we find character requisites such as blamelessness, monogamy, sobriety, good behavior, lack of covetousness. Right in the middle is this stipulation: "apt to teach" (v. 2). The only other qualification that could pass as a gift is "given to hospitality" (v. 2).

Apt to teach connotes a capacity for, potential for, disposal to, readiness for, fitness for, suitability to, inclination to—in other words, a gift for teaching.

Again, describing the servant of the Lord, Paul lists many character provisos, then turns to the gift of teaching. "The servant of the Lord must not strive; but be gentle unto all men, apt to

teach, patient, in meekness instructing those that oppose themselves" (2 Tim. 2:24, 25). Aptness at teaching is sandwiched
between character qualifications.

The *sine qua non* of Christian leadership is the teaching gift.
Ours is a reasoning faith. Worship demands the intellectual fac-
ulty. Renewal of life comes through renewal of mind, "But be ye
transformed by the renewing of your mind" (Rom. 12:2).
Growth in knowledge requires study of the great doctrines of the
faith concerning God, Christ, the Holy Spirit, man, salvation, church,
angels, demons, Satan, Scriptures, and eschatology (future events).
It involves serious inquiry into Scripture, both the Old Testament
and the New. To assist saints to learn God's truth, we need believers with the gift of teaching.

A Major Gift

Since growth in truth is so basic, so vital, and so continually essential for all believers from the newest to the most mature, it
would seem the gift of teaching must be given to many believers.
As stated earlier, teaching and prophecy are the only gifts listed
in all three catalogs of gifts.

Also, the gift should find outlet in a variety of ministries. Some
have the gift of teaching children, making an impact in the beginner and primary departments on successive waves of youngsters
who pass through their classes. Others have God-given ability to
rap with teen-agers. Still others find their most fruitful teaching
ministry on college campuses. Some communicate best with adults;
others in a seminary setting. Most teach at a particular, settled
location, but some are traveling Bible teachers.

Some exercise the gift best to large audiences. Others have
ability to teach the Word in small groups and in home Bible study
classes. Some may use the gift on a one-to-one basis, as Aquila
and Priscilla did, who, finding Apollos deficient in truth, invited
him home where they explained the Gospel more perfectly in a
private setting. Soloists and choirs can instruct through the talent
of music, "teaching and admonishing one another in psalms and
hymns and spiritual songs" (Col. 3:16). Women, though forbidden to teach with authority over men (1 Tim. 2:12), should
teach children and younger women (2 Tim. 1:5; 3:14, 15; Titus
2:4). Paul says the older women should be "teachers of good
things" (Titus 2:3).

Even if we all have not the gift of teaching, we are all to teach in a limited way. Recall the Spirit's rebuke, "When for the time ye ought to be teachers, ye have need that one teach you again which be the first principles of the oracles of God" (Heb. 5:12). These believers should have grown sufficiently to instruct others, but they were themselves in need of someone teaching them the ABC's of the faith. But note the sentence, "Ye ought to be teachers." Should not every believer teach someone else the fresh insights into biblical truth which he has acquired, warn of traps to be avoided, instruct in new lessons about Christ? Every believer is to be a teacher in his own quiet, confined way, even if he doesn't possess the gift to teach in formal situations. Fast growth of some congregations may be due in part to the informal teaching that goes on in open sharing services when many members participate.

If we are going to teach, whether or not we have the gift, we must first learn. The teaching gift was given to equip the saints for service so that they in turn could teach others. If we would be teachers, we must first be equipped by someone else's teaching. This means faithfully pursuing our opportunities for learning. Who cannot learn something from sermons, special meetings, Bible conferences? One pastor, in announcing the adult Sunday School department courses, used to say, "If you know everything there is to know about the Bible, you are excused!" Who of us is so far advanced that he is beyond learning something new?

Have we been lazy? Or have we been diligent? Have we gone to the Word daily? Do we know the teachings of the New Testament? Are we up on the main doctrines of the Christian faith? Have we asked for Holy Spirit illumination? More important, have we put into practice the precepts of God's Word? Paul spoke of those who desired to be teachers but who didn't understand what they were saying (1 Tim. 1:7).

If we have not refreshed our souls from the Scriptures, perhaps we should heed the warning, "Let not many of you become teachers" (James 3:1, *New American Standard Bible*). But if we let the Word of Christ dwell in us richly, we'll be prepared to teach others (Col. 3:16).

Paraphrasing the Apostle Paul, "Let the person possessing the gift of teaching devote himself to teaching" (Rom. 12:7).

9

The Gift of Exhortation

Roosters and preachers have many similarities, according to an anonymous and imaginative medieval source. For example, the rooster crows at certain hours; the preacher likewise. The rooster has a tendency to strut; the preacher also.

Perhaps this rooster-preacher comparison fits the concept many have of pulpiteers, especially those of the exhorting type. The exhorter, which office some denominations have, is often imagined high in a pulpit, alternately waving his arms or shaking a finger at the congregation, all the time shouting at the top of his lungs.

Is this what is meant by the gift of exhortation? (Rom. 12:8)

What is the Gift of Exhortation?
The word *exhort* in the original does not imply being bombastic, vociferous, thunderous. It may be translated comfort, console, entreat, beg, implore, counsel. In essence, it is *encouragement*.

Its noun form is a title for both the Holy Spirit and the Lord Jesus Christ. The Holy Spirit is called the Comforter (John 4:16); whereas the Lord Jesus is called Advocate (1 John 2:1). Both words could be translated *Paraclete,* which means *one called alongside to help.* The Holy Spirit has been called to our side to assist us; the Lord Jesus has been called to represent us before the Father.

The gift of exhortation involves the supernatural ability to come alongside to help, to strengthen the weak, reassure the wavering, buttress the buffeted, steady the faltering, console the troubled, encourage the halting. Just as the Holy Spirit is an instrument of help, so the Spirit uses this gift to make us instruments of encouragement to fellow saints.

A junior high advisor comes to the Christian Education Director after youth meeting one night ready to resign. The director listens sympathetically, then reminds the advisor that some lives have obviously been changed, and other young people are growing. He points out one or two areas that need correction and gives some suggestions to improve the group. After prayer the junior high advisor, instead of resigning, goes out with chin up, resolved to carry on and do a better job.

The ability to exhort is a gracious ability. It uses not so much sharp admonition as healing word. It works with compassion, not throwing a confessed sin back in the confessor's face. Without condoning the wrongdoing, the possessor of the gift of exhortation will help the victim see how he can overcome.

The gift is not so much exercised through public discourse, though this may be involved, as through personal counseling when one is called alongside in moments of misery. It may take time to encourage new believers, comfort the ill, counsel the perplexed, and strengthen the backslider.

Some New Testament Persons Who Had This Gift

Paul possessed the gift of exhortation. After starting several new churches on his first missionary journey, he retraced his steps "to Lystra, and to Iconium, and Antioch, confirming the souls of the disciples, and exhorting them to continue in the faith" (Acts 14: 21, 22). These new believers, left alone like orphans for several weeks or months, needed this encouragement from their spiritual father. Barnabas, Paul's companion on this tour, doubtless had the gift too.

Paul often exercised the gift of exhortation as he was bidding believers farewell. As he left Philippi, he comforted the new Christians there. Wouldn't one think that after his cruel beating and imprisonment the believers there should have been consoling him? But the Bible records that Paul did the comforting (Acts 16:40).

Again, after enduring a harrowing two-hour mob uproar at Ephesus, Paul comforted the Ephesian believers. Later versions translate "embraced" as "exhorted" (Acts 20:1). Again, Paul should perhaps have been the recipient of encouragement, but he did the strengthening, indicating the depth of his gift.

Paul's farewell speech to the Ephesian elders on his final visit was one of strong and long exhortation (Acts 20:17-35).

Judas and Silas, both prophets, also had the gift of exhortation. Assigned the task of delivering the verdict of the Jerusalem council—that Gentiles need not become Jews in order to be saved—they brought great comfort to the Antioch church. The encouragement factor is brought out twice in the context. The Antioch believers "rejoiced for the consolation [exhortation]. And Judas and Silas . . . exhorted the brethren with many words" (Acts 15:31, 32).

Peter exercised the gift, writing, "The elders which are among you I exhort . . . feed the flock" (1 Peter 5:1, 2). How natural that Peter should perform this ministry, for the Lord had commissioned him to "strengthen thy brethren" (Luke 22:32).

The writer of Hebrews wrote his epistle to encourage professing, persecuted Hebrew Christians not to go back to Judaism but to go on with Christ, who was far better than angels, Moses, Aaron, and the priesthood. He ended the letter, "And I beseech you, brethren, suffer the word of exhortation" (13:22).

As with most of the gifts, we are commanded to encourage others even though we may not possess this particular gift. Absence of a gift does not excuse disobedience.

Ten times in five verses (2 Cor. 1:3-7), one form or another of "exhortation" or "comfort" is used. God comforts us, not simply to make us comfortable, but so that we may comfort others.

Mutual encouragement is linked to church attendance. "Not forsaking the assembling of ourselves together, as the manner of some is, but exhorting one another" (Heb. 10:25). By our singing to each other admonishingly, by our testimonies during sharing time, by our very presence, we encourage each other.

Outstanding Example of Gift

Though many possessed the gift of exhortation in apostolic times, one New Testament character stands out as the epitome of this ability. If his original name were used, you probably would not recognize him. But Joses (is it familiar?) helped people so much that he was given a new name by the apostles. In fact, every time he appears in the sacred record he is encouraging someone. He so consistently used his gift that, according to Acts 4:36, the apostles called him "Barnabas, (which is, being interpreted, the son of consolation)."

Barnabas was a big brother, always helping. A survey of this man's ministry will illustrate how the gift of exhortation operates.

1. He helped needy saints.

The Early Church was composed of many common people and many poor. Confession of Christ made it harder to secure and hold employment. Perhaps some of the pilgrims from other nations who were converted in Jerusalem on the Day of Pentecost stayed there for fellowship and teaching, thus swelling the need for resources. Local believers had to help. Barnabas responded by selling property, probably on his native island of Cyprus, and surrendering the sale price at the apostles' feet to be used to alleviate temporal needs.

By giving tangible substance as well as verbal comfort, his act went beyond the gift of encouragement to that of showing mercy.

2. He endorsed an unwelcome convert.

Picture Paul's predicament after his conversion. He was rejected by the Sanhedrin, to whom his conversion came as bad news. His old friends considered him a renegade.

On the other hand, the people he had been rigorously persecuting, the Christians, were slow to receive this newcomer, suspicious of his motives. For one who had made such havoc of the church to suddenly become an ardent devotee to Christ seemed unbelievable. Had it not all happened some distance from Jerusalem, it might have seemed more credible.

The disciples were leery lest Paul infiltrate their ranks as a fifth columnist. Might his "conversion" not be a pretense designed for obtaining a full list of Christians to be rounded up for martyrdom?

The situation was touchy. Paul wished to labor in harmony with the church leaders, but they shrank from him lest he turn out to be a wolf in sheep's clothing. If he were rejected, though, might not Paul fade into oblivion, his great gifts lost to the cause of Christ? Or was he to start his own divisive movement?

Enter Barnabas. Discerning that God had been at work in Paul's life, Barnabas arranged a meeting with the leaders at Jerusalem, "brought him to the apostles, and declared unto them how he had seen the Lord in the way, and that He had spoken to him, and how he had preached boldly at Damascus in the name of Jesus"

(Acts 9:27). Barnabas sponsored Paul's cause with such success that the suspected newcomer "was with them coming in and going out at Jerusalem" (v. 28). What a boost Barnabas' gift must have given Paul!

3. *He accepted alien believers.*

Early believers, scattered by persecution, went everywhere preaching the Gospel, but mostly to Jews. However, some witnesses reared in the Hellenistic world shared the Gospel with the Gentiles at Antioch. The Lord blessed this witness, and a large number of Gentiles believed. The result was a seemingly irregular church, which the leaders at Jerusalem sent Barnabas to investigate.

After only a brief review, Barnabas rejoiced at the evidence of God's grace. Had he been a rigid, narrow-minded man, he might have squelched the new work as heretical, demanding that every Gentile acquiesce to the Law of Moses in order to gain acceptance in the church. But Barnabas' gift of encouragement, directed by the Spirit, enabled him to anticipate the verdict of the first church council by years.

He threw his full support into the work, staying over a year to help. It was here that believers were first called Christians. It was also the Antioch church which sent out the missionaries who first brought the Gospel to Europe. What far-reaching results from the faithful exercise of his gift of encouragement!

4. *He enlisted a promising teacher.*

The growing work at Antioch needed an expanded ministerial leadership. Barnabas recalled the young, zealous scholar whom he had endorsed to the church at Jerusalem. Paul's abilities to teach and preach would be just the answer. So, coveting a place of service for Paul, Barnabas set out to find him.

Paul's home city of Tarsus would be his likely abode. Here perhaps Paul had found refuge from the harassment of his Jerusalem countrymen who were exasperated at the loss of their champion to the hated "Way." Though doubtless engaged in some work, Paul had magnificent gifts which Barnabas now encouraged him to use at Antioch. So, Barnabas, with his ability to see potential in people, brought Paul as his helper.

Many young Christian workers need friends with the gift of encouragement. A young minister came to a New York City church. He didn't seem to do very well the first year. The deacons felt he had been a failure and should resign. However, one deacon spoke up: "Let's pray for him for a while, and let's all encourage him." They began to pray and encourage. He stayed another year. In fact, he stayed 42 years. He was Dr. Stuart MacArthur, pastor of the famed Calvary Baptist Church.

5. He developed a gifted assistant.

By trying to do it all himself and forgetting the dedicated teacher in Tarsus, Barnabas could have reigned as undisputed head at Antioch, for he had been dispatched by the apostles and the Jerusalem church. But the welfare of the church, not his own position, was his main interest. He must have known that Paul's abilities would ultimately place him in the ascendancy. The thought of one day ministering in Paul's shadow did not fluster Barnabas.

Bible students point out that on their first missionary journey the order reversed. No longer was it "Barnabas and Paul," but it became "Paul and Barnabas." Without envy on his part, Barnabas recognized the leadership of Paul. The senior member was willing to let the junior member take over top spot. A Christian has gone far in Christian grace when he can become assistant to his assistant, then carry on with the same enthusiasm. Someone wrote:

"It takes more grace than I can tell
To play the second fiddle well."

This was the third time Barnabas helped Paul. First, he endorsed him as an unwelcome convert. Second, he searched to find a not-too-busy but promising teacher. Third, he developed his assistant to become his senior. Not without reason has Barnabas been called "Mr. Greatheart."

6. He restored a youthful deserter.

Interestingly, the sharp argument that separated Paul and Barnabas stemmed from Barnabas' gift of encouragement. Recognizing in his nephew Mark a potential Christian leader just as he had in Paul, Barnabas had used his influence to have Mark taken on their first missionary journey as their assistant. But before the journey was half over, Mark defected. Whether homesick, afraid, noting Uncle Barnabas' leadership was gradually giving way to Paul's, or for some other reason, Mark returned home.

When the time came to start the next missionary tour, strong disagreement arose between Paul and Barnabas over taking John Mark with them. Paul thought of the work, Barnabas of the man. Paul operated on the principle—why endanger the work by the presence of a man who failed us last time? Barnabas thought,

Why should not this promising young man be given another chance?
Who was right will be debated through time. Perhaps the attitudes of both men were needed to do a job in depth on Mark. Paul's refusal made Mark realize that he would somehow have to redeem himself. Barnabas' encouragement, shown by his willingness to take Mark along even if it meant rupturing Paul's friendship, made Mark badly want to prove himself. Barnabas' willingness to give Mark another chance helped rescue him from his desertion. Barnabas saw Mark's potential for the ministry, which otherwise might have been wasted. Even if Mark were not prepared for the discipline of Paul's second missionary journey, Barnabas' gentler handling prepared him to become a good traveling companion for the Apostle Peter. Paul later acknowledged the merit of Mark, writing from prison in his last recorded letter, "Take Mark, and bring him with thee: for he is profitable to me for the ministry" (2 Tim. 4:11).

Do we realize that had not Barnabas used his gift of encouragement we might be missing half the New Testament books? Through his salvaging of Mark, he got us a writer of one of the four Gospels, possibly the first one written. Through his cultivation of Paul, he got us the writer of 13 epistles. Here is something remarkable. Barnabas never wrote a book that found its way into the sacred canon, but he encouraged two men who between them wrote 14 books, over half of the 27 New Testament volumes. How much we owe this self-effacing exhorter!

Laymen little realize how much they can buoy up their pastor's spirits through the gift of encouragement. In a struggling church with less than 100 in the morning service, the Easter attendance reached 150. The pastor commented to a member, "Do you think we'll ever have this many again?"

"Of course," replied the optimistic member. "We'll have this crowd every week."

The wavering pastor took heart, redoubled his efforts. Today the church averages 400 on Sunday mornings.

A man who exemplified the gift of encouragement came into my life in 1956. I had heard of Rev. Leymon W. Ketcham, better known as "Deak," from my college days, when he was the star basketball player for The King's College. Though I had once heard him preach and once had a short phone conversation with him, I had never met him.

One Sunday morning a fine family visited our church, taking seats near the front. Something clicked. I recognized him. That was the beginning of one of the warmest friendships my wife and I have ever experienced. I discovered "Deak" to be a bulwark, a solid rock, always helpful, a great encourager.

When I spoke in The King's College chapel service, where he served as vice-president, he encouraged me to put the message in print. Because of his advocacy I submitted a manuscript which was later published—my first book. He was also indirectly responsible for the publication of another of my manuscripts.

In personal conversations when I expressed some reservation about some church program, he, in his quiet, steady, winsome manner would point out its good points and urge its continuation. I recall, when our new Sunday School addition was almost completed, mentioning that our church needed greater evangelistic zeal. His immediate reply was, "This building is an expression of the church's desire to witness."

"Deak" became Director of Development for Gordon College and Seminary four years later. In 1966 he became terminally ill. Though in deep discomfort he continued to encourage people from his hospital bed. He asked me if I would preach his funeral service. I began the sermon that day in the crowded Gordon Chapel, "As a boy I used to wonder—where does a pastor go for strength and inspiration? The pastor encourages others—where does he receive his encouragement? The orthodox answer is that he gets it from the Lord. But 10 years ago I found an additional answer. Not only from God but also through a man sent from God did I receive strength. Ten years ago I became Deak's pastor, but really he has been my pastor." To me, "Deak" had been a pillar of strength because he used his gift of exhortation.

10

The Gifts
of Knowledge
and of Wisdom

Knowledge differs from wisdom.

Knowledge is information. Wisdom is the right use of information to achieve proper ends.

A man studies hard to become a certified public accountant. Then he uses his knowledge to juggle company accounts to embezzle. This improper use of his expertise betrays lack of wisdom.

When you fly these days, before you board the plane you are subjected to detection devices and your hand luggage to thorough search. Our scientific genius has designed planes which can fly at nearly 600 miles an hour carrying 300 persons or more across country in five hours or less. But we cannot prevent hijacking without this embarrassing, even humiliating scrutiny. The knowledge explosion has given us a super-ample fund of facts, but where is the wisdom to correlate and control this vast reservoir of information?

The first two gifts mentioned by Paul in the list in 1 Corinthians 12 are wisdom and knowledge. "For to one is given by the Spirit the word of wisdom; to another the word of knowledge by the same Spirit" (v. 8). Since these gifts are closely related, both will be handled in this chapter, though in reverse order, knowledge first, then wisdom in greater length.

The Word of Knowledge
The gift of the word of knowledge is the charisma which enables the believer to search, systematize, and summarize the teachings

of the Word of God. Through it, the Christian is enabled to acquire deep insight into divine truth. This supernatural ability brings illumination of God's thoughts not discoverable by human reason.

Since knowledge helps others only when communicated, Paul speaks of the *word* or *utterance* of knowledge. This ability is closely related to the gift of teaching. In fact, some scholars consider *teaching* and *utterance of knowledge* one and the same gift. However, in our lists the gifts are classified as separate. In the gift of teaching, emphasis is on communication or *utterance;* in the gift under discussion, emphasis is on *knowledge.*

In the anti-intellectual atmosphere of our day when many seek experience more than truth, we need to emphasize the importance of knowledge in the Christian faith. Of course, this is not knowledge at the expense of experience, but rather knowledge which directs zeal.

Dr. John R. W. Stott, Bible teacher at several Inter-Varsity Urbana conventions, pointed out in a recent lecture series at Gordon College titled, "Your Mind Matters," that four Christian doctrines support the need for thinking and the importance of knowledge. The doctrine of creation teaches that man, because he is made in God's image, is a rational being. The doctrine of revelation implies the ability of man to grasp God's thoughts. The doctrine of redemption involves renewal of our minds. Finally, the doctrine of judgment states that knowledge is one factor by which God will judge us. To belittle the mind is to undercut these four major Christian doctrines.

Think of the large place Paul gave knowledge in his ministry in Ephesus. For two years he argued daily in the hall of Tyrannus. A marginal reading in certain manuscripts adds the words, "from the fifth hour to the tenth" (Acts 19:9). Five hours a day for two years would total 3650 hours of teaching. No wonder "all they which dwelt in Asia heard the Word of the Lord" (v. 10). Utterance of knowledge gave content to evangelism and edified those won so that they, not Paul, fanned out into all the provinces to carry the Gospel. This episode has been called one of the most amazing illustrations of the equipping of the saints for the ministry —and it couldn't have been done without the word of knowledge.

Whether or not we have this gift, we are all called to "grow" in grace, and in the knowledge of our Lord and Saviour Jesus Christ" (2 Peter 3:18). Paul's prayer for the Corinthians was that they might be "enriched by Him, in all utterance, and in all knowledge" (1 Cor. 1:5). He prayed for the Colossians that they "might be filled with the knowledge of His will in all wisdom and spiritual understanding" (Col. 1:9).

The two major theological words of the Reformation, Melanchthon's *Loci Communes Rerum Theologicarum,* which went through 30 editions before the author's death and was used for decades later as a textbook of didactic theology in Lutheran universities, and Calvin's *Institutes,* were produced by lay theologians. Neither Melanchthon nor Calvin was ordained by human hands. You don't have to be a professional clergyman to have the gift of knowledge.

The Word of Wisdom
The story is told of an American on his way home from Europe by boat after graduating from a continental university. He was on deck examining his four years of notes when a sudden roll of the boat pitched him against the rail and propelled his notes overboard. He was not injured, but he had to go back to Europe for four more years to gain more notes!

Such knowledge is useless. And even knowledge stored in the mind is useless unless it is applied. This principle pertains to divine knowledge too. It's not enough to be able to grasp and systemize the deep truths of God's Word. Also needed is the ability to relate those truths to the needs and problems of life. This is the area in which the gift of the word of wisdom operates. The ability to apply knowledge to vexing situations, to weigh their true nature, to exercise spiritual insight into the rightness or wrongness of a complex state of affairs calls for the gift of wisdom.

Here are four major areas in which wisdom uses knowledge to achieve proper ends.

1. Defense before hostile courts.

Jesus promised His disciples that when they came before councils, courts, and kings for His name they would not need to make advance preparation for their defense. What to say would be given them by the Holy Spirit (Matt. 10:19, 20). Such difficult situations would require wisdom at that needy moment. (Note that this promise does not pertain to preparation of Sunday School lessons or sermons.)

The Acts gives several instances of God's provision of wisdom under these circumstances, such as Peter's two defenses before the Sanhedrin (Acts 4:8ff.; 5:29ff.). The first time, the council, perceiving that the apostles were "unlearned and ignorant men," marvelled. The second time, cut to the heart by Peter's answer, they took counsel to slay the apostles but ended up by beating them.

When Stephen disputed with Jewish leaders, "they were not able to resist the wisdom and the spirit by which he spake" (6:10). Later, before the Sanhedrin, his defense was characterized by such wisdom that the only answer the council could give was stoning (7:54ff.).

Paul, among those who heard Stephen's defense, could never forget. Doubtless, Stephen's words of wisdom were goads which prodded Paul till the day he kicked against them no more (9:5). After his conversion, Paul spoke with the same gift of wisdom, and "confounded the Jews which dwelt at Damascus, proving that this is very Christ" (9:22). Back in Jerusalem, before the same Sanhedrin of which he had been a member and with whom he had listened to Stephen, "he spake boldly in the name of the Lord Jesus, and disputed" so unanswerably that they went about to slay him (9:29).

Through his long and stormy career, Paul was called on to make several defenses: before the raging mob at Jerusalem (22:1ff.), before the Sanhedrin (23:1ff.), before Felix (24:10ff.), before Festus (25:6ff.), and before Agrippa and Bernice (26:1ff.). On every occasion, whether defending the resurrection, recounting his conversion, giving the Gospel, or appealing to his hearers, he certainly evidenced the gift of the utterance of wisdom.

This gift of wisdom is needed today by believers living where persecution occurs. *Eternity* magazine says that more than 600 Baptists have been imprisoned in Russia in the past decade for their faith. One of them, Georgi Zheltonozke was charged with receiving and distributing Bibles, New Testaments, and other spiritual literature, thereby trampling on Soviet laws, and with conducting prayer meetings in his home. Though found guilty and sentenced to three years in a Siberian labor camp, this middle-aged Russian Baptist evidenced the gift of wisdom at his trial. Here is some of the dialogue:

Judge: "Did you import and distribute literature?"
Georgi: "Yes, and I gave it to everybody."

Judge: "Where is it printed?"

Georgi: "Praise God, I don't know."

Judge: "Why did you do this?"

Georgi: "According to Lenin's decree on religion, citizens are permitted not only to believe, but also to confess their faith and propagate it. Lenin granted freedom, he didn't limit it; the same is true of the United Nations declaration of human rights."

At this point Georgi complained to the judge about the coarse behavior of Soviet officials who broke up a prayer meeting he had organized. Some were drunk, and they insulted the believers, calling them a rabble.

Judge: "If I read my Romans right, I find at 13:2 it says 'Obey the authorities.' "

Georgi: "The answer to that is Ephesians 6:12: 'We are not contending against flesh and blood but against the principalities, against the powers, against the world rulers of this present darkness.' Whom should we obey, man or God? The lesser yields to the greater. I submit to God; to whom do you submit?"

Given opportunity to speak in his own defense, he said, "You are trying me for my faith and not for breaking the law. Our faith cannot be contained only in a church building. Faith without works is dead, as a body is dead without the spirit."

He accused the authorities of not allowing children to be brought up in a Christian spirit. "You start educating children into Communist movements. We have to train our children too, because when they grow up it may be too late to tell them about God. I lost 27 years before being converted, and I don't want to see them do the same" (*Eternity*, November 1972).

2. Answer to unbelievers' arguments.

All believers are commanded to "be ready always to give an answer to every man that asketh you a reason of the hope that is in you with meekness and fear" (1 Peter 3:15). However, some have a special ability to meet the attacks and to refute the arguments of unbelievers.

Our Lord, who had the Spirit without measure, had this ability. Repeatedly He refuted those who tried to trap Him. They asked if it were lawful to pay taxes to Caesar or not. He gave the memorable answer, "Render therefore unto Caesar the things which are Caesar's; and unto God the things that are God's" (Matt. 22:21). The Sadducees, who didn't believe in the resurrection, came forth with their imaginary stock story about a woman who married seven brothers one after another, then asked whose wife she would be in the resurrection. His answer amazed and stumped them (Luke 20:39, 40). Then Jesus went on the offensive, asking the Pharisees how the Messiah could be both David's Lord and son. The result: "No man was able to answer Him a word, neither durst any man from that day forth ask Him any more questions" (Matt. 22:46).

Paul exercised the gift of wisdom as he disputed at Athens in the synagogue and on Mars Hill (Acts 17:17ff.), as he reasoned with his kinsmen at Ephesus (18:19), later "disputing and persuading the things concerning the kingdom of God" (19:8). In fact, Paul's customary approach to the Jews was to find a synagogue, then to reason "with them out of the Scriptures, opening and alleging, that Christ must needs have suffered, and risen again from the dead; and that this Jesus, whom I preach unto you, is Christ" (17:2, 3).

Evangelistic preaching requires some "wisdom" content such as evidence for the deity of Christ and reasons for belief in the resurrection of Christ.

Ability to answer critical attacks helps remove stumbling blocks which might hamper non-Christians from serious consideration of the claims of Christ. This discipline is called *apologetics,* which comes from a word meaning "defense." The field of apologetics, which helps Christians subdue doubts, may have more value for confirming the church than for converting the world.

Men with the apologetic wisdom gift would include famed defender of the faith, Dr. J. Gresham Machen, whose *The Virgin Birth of Christ* is still an unassailable classic, and Dr. Francis Schaeffer, author of many works which show the rationality and relevance of historic Christianity amidst the prevalent skepticism, existentialism, and irrationalism of our day.

3. Solution to problem situations.

Though all who lack wisdom are told to ask for it (James 1:5), some have special ability to resolve dilemmas.

When Solomon was faced with the dilemma of choosing which of two women was the rightful mother of one surviving baby, he certainly required the divine wisdom with which God had just endowed him (1 Kings 3:16-28).

The first recorded church conflict was potentially explosive, as

Grecian widows claimed neglect in the daily dispensing of food. The church appointed seven men "full of the Holy Ghost and wisdom" (Acts 6:3) to settle the matter. As a prisoner at Caesarea and a veteran of two hearings, Paul faced the difficult decision whether to return to Jerusalem for trial or appeal to Caesar, which meant going to hostile Rome. Paul needed the gift of wisdom, for if he returned to Jerusalem he would risk losing his life in ambush by the men determined to kill him. If he chose Rome, he might be executed. Yet he would achieve his ambition, also God's plan, of preaching in the great capital. Paul chose the second alternative. He received an expense-free trip to Rome, wrote four epistles while there, and won countless numbers to Christ, including soldiers from Caesar's household (Acts 25:9-11).

Saints were forbidden to go to law against fellow saints. For a believer to adjudicate fairly, he would need special wisdom. Paul wrote, "Is it so, that there is not a wise man among you? No, not one that shall be able to judge between his brethren?" (1 Cor. 6:5)

You're in a church business meeting, or board or committee session. The group has reached an impasse on the matter under discussion. The members seem hopelessly divided. Then someone stands to his feet, quotes a Scriptural principle and applies it to the situation. Suddenly the answer comes. Everyone agrees. A word of wisdom may shorten debate by casting light on a problem and providing objectivity. The decision then reached becomes virtually unanimous because it is based on common insight.

Incidentally, the gift of wisdom does not create confusion, envy, or strife, but rather comes with gentleness, mercy, and peace (James 3:15-18).

Corrie ten Boom in her book, *The Hiding Place,* tells of incident after incident in her daring underground activity that required divine wisdom. For example, should a certain young man be trusted? If he were an informer, all the teamwork thus far painstakingly built up would be dashed to pieces in a moment. But this young man had risked his safety to give warning. Corrie ten Boom prayed aloud for guidance. As assurance about this man came, she wondered how long she would be led by the gift of wisdom.

4. Application to practical conduct.

Both knowledge and wisdom do not necessarily reside in the same person. A person may be able to perceive the system of truth contained in the Word, yet lack the ability to apply these insights to life. Wisdom involves the gift of putting knowledge to work in daily experience.

Most of Paul's epistles are built on this two-sided base of knowledge and wisdom. For example, the first half of Ephesians presents deep truths about the high and holy calling of the church. Then the second half applies these teachings to various life situations, such as the home (husbands, wives, parents, children), employment (masters, servants), speech, anger, honesty, industry, kindness, sobriety, and joyful thanksgiving. The outline of Ephesians might be: knowledge (1—3); wisdom (4—6).

A bushman in Australia was taught to write. A week later he forged a check. He had knowledge but lacked wisdom. The Bible lays down many principles. These may be applied to family life, money, relation to government, amusements, x-rated movies, social life, to name a few. Perhaps more evangelicals are needed with the gift of wisdom to apply the theoretical teachings of the Word of God to every area of daily life.

An editorial in *Christianity Today* attempts to apply biblical truth to the worship of sports today, particularly football. Reminding us that Tertullian, an early Christian theologian and moralist, warned against gladiatorial combats, the editorial asks, "If Tertullian were to return and visit late 20th-century America . . . he would find that the combats, gradually abolished after the conversion of the Emperor Constantine, have no counterpart in modern life. Or would he? We have no gladiators . . . but we do have 'combats,' most notably pro football, which columnist Carl Rowan calls our nation's 'new religion,' and which reaches its climax with the January Super Bowl. An Atlanta *Journal Consitution* writer commented last fall, 'Empty pews dot the beautiful churches on Peachtree Street. There will be no empty seats at the Atlanta Stadium.'

"When Christians were present in the arenas of the Roman Empire, it was usually as victims for the wild beasts. The presence of Christians at modern-day spectacles is ordinarily much less painful. Yet modern spectacles, like those of Tertullian's day, may represent a temptation and a danger for Christians. When a Green Bay minister can say of his city, 'Everyone's schedule—every family, every church—is determined by the playing of the Green Bay Packers,' then something is wrong with our priorities. 'Six days shalt thou labor,' said the Lord, and He did not add, 'but the seventh is reserved for spectacles' " (Copyright 1973, *Christianity Today*).

Though the gift of the utterance of wisdom is sovereignly assigned to a limited number, the rest of us need to pray that God will give us the "Spirit of wisdom" (Eph. 1:17).

Part III
The
Serving
Gifts

11

The Gift of Helps

A young Christian in Seattle, Wash., saw a man handing out tracts in a busy, downtown area. The distributor had a satchel full of tracts which he gave out rapidly without stopping to engage in conversation. *Why doesn't he talk with someone?* thought the observing Christian. *His method is so cold and impersonal.*

Finally, unable to stand it any longer, the young Christian approached the distributor from behind. Turning him around by his collar and looking directly into his face, he asked, "Why don't you speak to someone about the Saviour?"

The fellow blurted out, "Ugh—ugh—ugh!" He couldn't speak. He was a mute. But he was doing what he could.

In chapter 3, we said the gifts can be divided into two major categories: speaking and serving. Peter said, "If any man speak, let him speak as the oracles of God; if any man minister [sometimes translated *serve*], let him do it as of the ability which God giveth" (1 Peter 4:11). Many believers, who lack speaking gifts, have serving gifts.

Having completed the speaking gifts, we now turn to the serving gifts, first of which is the gift of helps.

What Is the Gift of Helps?

The gift of helps (listed in 1 Cor. 12:28) carries the meaning of assistance, lending a hand. Its verb form was used by Paul when he told us to *support* the weak (Acts 20:35). An intensive verb form of the same word was spoken by exasperated Martha, left alone to prepare dinner, when she asked Jesus, "Dost Thou not care that my sister hath left me to serve alone? Bid her therefore that she help me" (Luke 10:40). *Help* here means literally, "to take one's turn with." Martha wanted Mary to do her stint in the kitchen.

The gift of helps is generally considered the same as the gift of ministering (Rom. 12:7). An example of this gift may be seen in the growing Early Church. The Grecian element complained against the Hebrew sector, claiming their widows were neglected in the daily distribution of food. The archenemy of the church was taking double aim at the infant fellowship, both by creating dissension, and, even more significant, by turning the apostles from their divinely appointed ministry to lesser tasks. But with divine insight the Twelve resisted the temptation, asserting it would be a mistake for them to neglect the Word of God to wait on tables (Acts 6:2). They solved the problem by having the church elect seven capable, spiritual men to take over the business of welfare distribution. Their gift of helps was not in waiting on tables, though it did involve that, but was the freeing of the apostles to major in the Word of God and prayer. The distribution of food is an incidental factor. The essence of the gift is that the temporal help given, whether waiting on tables or whatever, enables a Christian worker to devote more time to a spiritual ministry.

The gift of helps is the Spirit-given ability to serve the church in any supporting role, usually temporal, though sometimes spiritual. The gift enables one to serve joyfully and diligently wherever and whenever required. Those served have more time and energy for the ministry of prayer and preaching, resulting in the blessing of others. After the election of these seven deacons, historian Luke comments, "The Word of God increased; and the number of the disciples multiplied in Jerusalem greatly" (v. 7).

This gift is not for helping the poor, sick, aged, orphans, and widows (which is really the gift of showing mercy), but for lending a hand wherever it will release other workers in their spiritual ministries, and to do it in such a way that it strengthens and heartens. Said one pastor, "I have never mimeographed a page in my 30 years in the pastorate." His refusal to mimeograph does not stem from any aversion to soiling his hands but from dislike of devoting valuable minutes to tasks which could be done by members of the church. "When I have been trained to minister the Bible from pulpit and in private interview, why should I give valuable time to what many others could do so capably and willingly? Their gift of helps has furthered my ministry."

Other Biblical Examples

On their first missionary journey, Paul and Barnabas had John Mark as their helper or minister (Acts 13:5). Doubtless he performed many menial, temporal tasks, freeing them to carry on their evangelistic and edifying ministries.

Luke speaks of two men, Timotheus and Erastus, who ministered to Paul (Acts 19:22). These men with their gift of helps, Paul sent into Macedonia to be of help there.

In fact, Paul gathered about him a full team of workers without whom he could not possibly have carried on his great ministry. Luke, the beloved physician, must have been a valuable assistant, especially at the time of beatings, stonings, and other privations. Luke often lists others who exercised the gift of helps (Acts 20:4).

At the end of his letters, Paul sometimes mentions several faithful helpers (Rom. 16:3ff.; Col. 4:7ff.). The Romans list contains 26 names, of whom perhaps 10 are women, most of whom are commended directly or indirectly for being helpers. The first person mentioned in the chapter is specifically singled our for the gift of helps or ministering. Paul says, "I commend unto you Phebe our sister, which is a servant of the church which is at Cenchrea . . . for she hath been a succourer of many, and of myself also" (Rom. 16:1, 2). The word *servant* means *minister*.

At the end of 1 Corinthians, Paul writes about the household of Stephanas, who "addicted themselves to the ministry of the saints" (16:15). Here's a noble kind of addiction—devotion to serving others. Writing to the Philippians, Paul singles out Epaphroditus who "ministered to my wants" (2:25).

When runaway slave Onesimus was converted, he began to use his gift of helps to minister to Paul in prison, who termed him "profitable . . . to me" (Phile. 11). So that Onesimus might be profitable to his master, Paul sent him back to exercise his gift of helpfulness to Philemon.

During his final imprisonment, Paul wanted Timothy to minister helpfully by coming to visit him before winter and bringing cloak and books which Paul had left elsewhere. He also asked Mark to come. Now a proven soldier of the cross, he was profitable to Paul "for the ministry" (2 Tim. 4:11). Remember—the gift of ministering is the gift of helps.

Bible commentators have long puzzled over the meaning of the seven stars connected with the seven churches of Revelation (1:20). Stated to be the seven angels of the seven churches, many believe them to be the pastors. On the other hand, since the word "angel" also means "messenger," some hold that these seven were the ones who carried the messages to the seven churches from John on the Isle of Patmos. If so, they ministered helpfully by transporting these letters to their proper destinations.

Current Examples

Potential outlets for exercise of the gift of helps seem almost unlimited. The ultimate end of helps is the edification of others. Christian workers, released from temporal tasks, can concentrate more on their spiritual priorities.

Someone prepares the handwork and does the cutouts for a busy Vacation Bible School teacher. The helper, perhaps possessing no teaching gift, uses her serving gift to free the teacher, helping her use her speaking gift more effectively.

A Sunday School class member secures the textbooks, arranges the chairs, brings in the chalkboard or cassette player, handles the records, takes the offering, hands out take-home papers at the end. The teacher has been released from menial but necessary jobs to devote more time to teaching.

Office records, bookkeeping, serving as treasurer, dictation, typing, filing, preparing a mailing, delivery of church flowers after Sunday services to someone sick, ushering, taping of Christian broadcasts, maintenance and repair of church facilities, preparing the elements for the Lord's Supper, driving the pastor to the airport, meeting some special speaker at the station, all these contribute definitely to the upbuilding of the saints by freeing the leaders for the spiritual ministries to which they have been called.

One minister who broadcasts several times a year has his rough manuscripts typed in finished form by housewives who formerly worked in offices. Another clergyman, while reading privately, marks passages he wishes copied, gives the books to volunteers who type copies of all marked paragraphs for his files. No pastor or church staff member can do it all. How necessary to accept help graciously from those who have the gift of ministering.

Those who work in missionary society offices free missionaries for their main calling. Those who go out to the field in supporting roles likewise liberate missionaries. The director of a youth camp in Japan wrote, "The Lord sent us five college-age young people to assist in summer camps this year. These young people washed dishes, taught English during Japanese-English camp, worked in the crafts room and the store, taught water-skiing, served as life guards, assisted in the recreational activities, and shared in the music. They had a general idea of what would be expected of them prior to coming to the camp, but I guess we forgot to include in the job description the fact that they might have to help dig a hole for a 500-gallon fuel tank and then help tar that tank on a windblown, snowy day."

Short Terms Abroad, an organization which serves mission boards by recruiting personnel for short term service, in its latest 70-page listing, catalogs 5,600 openings in 157 mission societies under 132 job titles, such as accountants, business managers, lawyers, secretaries, agriculturists, mechanics, pilots, teachers, engineers, artists, editors, photographers, printers, writers, dentists, dental hygienists and technicians, doctors, lab technicians, nurses, optometrists, pharmacists, physiotherapists, X-ray technicians, music teachers, intrumentalists, vocalists, radio announcers and technicians, news directors, program producers, script writers, builders, carpenters, mason workers, cooks, electricians, heavy equipment operators, housekeepers, maintenance men, painters, plumbers, surveyors, truck drivers, waitresses, camp directors and workers, houseparents, recreational directors, and water safety directors. Hundreds of believers who never thought they would ever serve overseas are now helping in their own specialized areas. To the extent they disengage missionaries from temporal occupations to preach and teach, they are employing the gift of helps.

Dr. Charles W. Anderson, president of Northeastern Bible College and for 33 years pastor of Brookdale Baptist Church, Bloomfield, N.J., tells of a lady who walked into church one Sunday decked out like a Christmas tree, all furs and feathers and baubles. She had led a checkered life, with more than one marriage and involvement in strange religious experiences, but she found the Lord and really straightened out. Wanting to do something for the Lord, she witnessed to her Jewish husband. She told Dr. Anderson that the night her husband became a Christian she would kneel on the church floor and kiss the very spot where he was converted. Sure enough, the night he accepted Christ, she walked forward behind him, knelt down before the congregation and kissed the very floor where her husband prayed to receive Christ.

In gratitude to God, she wanted to be used of the Lord in the best way she knew how. She didn't know how to get started. She heard about tract distribution so installed a large tract rack in her vestibule with hundreds and hundreds of tracts. Anyone coming to the door received a tract of one kind or another.

Then she thought that perhaps God could use her in playing the piano in outreach services of the church. But realizing that a piano cannot be carried around, she learned to play the accordion well enough to play a few hymns at street meetings and hospital services.

Then she got to thinking about young people in the church who should have been involved in such activities. She told them that she would teach them how to play the accordion at no charge if they would promise to play it for the Lord. She rounded up 20 to 30 youngsters, 9 to 12 years of age, who bought accordions. Deciding she could not go to their homes to teach them every week, she decided to give lessons over the phone every Saturday morning beginning at 8 o'clock. She would spend 15 minutes with Mary, then 15 minutes with Jimmy, then Sally. She would get them to play their lessons over the phone, listen, evaluate their progress, and help correct their mistakes.

Dr. Anderson says, "It wasn't very long before she had quite a little band going. We used them one Sunday evening. Everyone thought they were terrific. Jack Wyrtzen heard about them and used them on his radio program. All this because of a woman who often said, 'I don't have any talents but I'll just do what I can for God, and maybe He can do something with it.' God surely used her gift." Among other benefits, her gift of helps released the director of music for his many other ministries.

In a sense, the ministry of private intercession is a gift of helps. Earlier we stated that the gift of helps usually involves temporal assistance, though sometimes spiritual. Paul urged the Corinthians, "Ye also helping together by prayer for us" (2 Cor. 1:11). Who can ever measure, this side of eternity, how much blessing has anointed the public ministries of pastors and missionaries as a result of the prayer help of the saints—sometimes bedridden, insignificant, uneducated, or poor—who stood by faithfully in the quiet of their own rooms?

A young minister, just settled in his first pastorate in Philadelphia, was visited by some of his godly members. "You do not seem to be a strong preacher," they said. "In the normal course of affairs, perhaps you'd fail. But a small group of us are going to meet every Sunday morning before the services to pray for you." The group grew to more than a thousand persons. The pastor became one of America's finest preachers and a world-renowned evangelist, Dr. J. Wilbur Chapman, helped by prayer.

Preparing meals for God's servants is certainly a ministry of helps. How many godly women, like Martha, have labored out of love in the kitchen so that the resultant dinner could further the outreach of God's Word? My mother, who could not speak in public nor give a verbal testimony, but whose life was one of exemplary godliness, liked to entertain God's servants. Time and time again she would have visiting preachers for dinner, or youth Gospel team members overnight, or a missionary for several days.

After Mother passed away, I found in her dresser drawer a page, yellowed with time, the only piece of writing among all her effects. It was a poem titled "A Martha," said to have been written by an unknown girl of 19 in 1928. Through preserving these words my mother seemed to say, "I couldn't speak or teach in public, but I did try to serve my Lord in menial ways." Here are the words on the faded paper:

> "Lord of all pots and pans and things;
> Since I've no time to be
> A saint by doing lovely things,
> Or watching late with Thee,
> Or dreaming in the dawnlight,
> Or storming heaven's gates,
> Make me a saint by getting meals,
> And washing up the plates.
>
> "Although I must have Martha's hands,
> I have a Mary mind;
> And when I black the boots and shoes,
> Thy sandals, Lord, I find.

I think of how they trod the earth,
What time I scrub the floor;
Accept this meditation, Lord,
I haven't time for more.

"Warm all the kitchen with Thy love,
And light it with Thy peace;
Forgive me all my worrying,
And make all grumbling cease.
Thou who didst love to give men food,
In room, or by the sea,
Accept this service that I do—
I do it unto Thee."

12

The Gift of Hospitality

A postman from Oregon and his wife recently traveled halfway across the country to a strange city where she was to be hospitalized. The only people they knew there were a young professor and his wife who had worshiped briefly in the postman's home church more than five years before.

Reports the postman, "During the first week, my wife received good care in the hospital. People we had not known before opened their homes to me so that each of my nights was spent in the warmth of Christian love and fellowship. I stayed in three different homes and had a place to lodge for as long as we were in that city. One woman baked a birthday cake for my wife, though they had never met until the cake was presented at the hospital ("I Was a Stranger," *Eternity*).

The advantages to the postman—no lonely motel and less expense. The benefits to his wife—she knew she had friends in the city praying for her, and her birthday was brightened. The dividends to the hosts—they discovered anew that it is more blessed to give than to receive, that entertaining strangers brings its rewards.

The postman speculates that his experience was more the exception than the rule. Perhaps the families he contacted were more dedicated or more comfortably situated to help than the average Christian is. He asks these basic questions, "Why were these homes opened to me? And why was I bold enough to present my need for Christian love and support?" In answer he points out that the Bible has much to say on this matter. We are to bear each other's burdens, to do good to all men, especially to the household of fellow believers, and to practice hospitality.

Peter commands us, "Use hospitality one to another without grudging" (1 Peter 4:9). Amplification might read, "Gladly open up your homes and welcome each other as guests, especially those who need a meal or a room overnight—and don't complain about the inconvenience."

Though hospitality is not included in any of Paul's lists of gifts, the context in which hospitality is mentioned seems to earn it consideration as a separate gift. After Peter speaks of hospitality in verse 9, he immediately goes on in the next two verses to say that whatever gift a person has should be faithfully exercised. The link in Peter's thinking between hospitality and gifts strongly implies that hospitality is a gift.

What It Is
Hospitality is frequently commanded in the New Testament. Paul wants all believers to be "given to hospitality" (Rom. 12:13). Especially he requires an elder to be a "lover of hospitality" (Titus 1:8; 1 Tim. 3:2).

A widow could qualify for relief funds from the church treasury if, among other stipulations, "she have lodged strangers" (1 Tim. 5:10).

The writer of Hebrews enjoins, "Be not forgetful to entertain strangers" (13:2).

The main part of the word *hospitality* is hospital. Ancient travelers, whether pilgrims or businessmen, fared poorly when venturing beyond their own country. Thus, religious leaders established international guest houses in the fifth century. These havens were called "hospice" from *hospes,* Latin for "guests." With the coming of the Crusades, the importance of the hospice increased greatly. Pilgrims, crusaders, and other travelers found hospices, by this time run by religious orders, the only reputable guest houses of the era. Soon after the Crusades most of these institutions began to specialize in the care of the poor, sick, aged, and crippled. During the 15th century, secular interests took over most entertaining of travelers, so the *hospital* restricted its function to care and treatment of the sick and handicapped. But originally it meant a haven for guests.

Though all believers are to be hospitable, some, perhaps more women then men, possess a special ability. The gift of hospitality is that supernatural ability to provide open house and warm welcome for those in need of food and lodging. Those who possess this gift should cultivate it.

Need for Hospitality

For the Early Church to begin to get the Gospel out to the ends of the world required travel. In addition, business pursuits took many believers to all parts of the Roman Empire. Though the empire was known for its good roads, finding suitable places to stay was difficult. No Holiday Inns, Howard Johnsons, Hiltons, or Sheratons dotted the highways. Since robbers and other dangers lurked along the way, since ancient inns were often nothing but brothels, and since most itinerant preachers were poor, Christians were exhorted to open their homes and welcome as guests those bearing the Good News. Thus, hospitality furthered the Gospel.

When our Lord sent the 70 out, He expected them to be entertained. When the apostles and their fellow workers were commanded to take the Gospel to remote places, the Lord of the harvest anticipated open-heartedness on the part of believers. Many traveling Christians carried letters of commendation. Not only did the traveler look to a Christian home for hospitality, but scattered believers looked to the traveler to bring word of Christ's work in other places, fostering a sense of unity throughout the world. Thus, hospitality was indispensable both to the entertained and the entertainer. This practice, admired by the heathen, drew favor for the Christian cause.

Perhaps the need for hospitality for traveling Christian workers does not exist in the same degree today. Excellent motels can be found almost anywhere, and they are often preferred by evangelists, missionaries, and Bible teachers for study purposes and for privacy. But blessing can accrue to homes that invite God's servants for food and fellowship, where needs exist.

Traveling groups from Christian schools and organizations, such as choirs and drama clubs, usually require of every host church an evening meal, overnight lodging, breakfast, and a bag lunch. Imagine the motel and food bill for a 40-voice choir on a 10-day tour! Yes, the need for Christian hospitality still exists.

Also, in every church is a host of lonely believers whose hearts are hungry for fellowship, despite appearance of contentment.

Examples

In many congregations today, one or more families with an extra apartment or an extra bedroom with private bath take special delight in entertaining guest evangelists, Bible teachers, and missionaries. These gracious hosts know when to engage their guest in conversation and when to let him meditate by himself. They have the knack of making him feel at home. This practice of hospitality goes back to earliest New Testament days.

Though our Lord spent many a night on the mountain praying, He was a welcome guest in several homes, especially that of Mary, Martha, and Lazarus in the Bethany area.

Peter lodged "many days in Joppa with one Simon a tanner" (Acts 9:43). Peter received an invitation, which he doubtless accepted, to "tarry certain days" as a guest in the home of centurion Cornelius (Acts 10:48).

Paul and his team must have been guests in other peoples' homes most nights during his missionary journeys. Lydia, seller of purple at Philippi, urged Paul, "If ye have judged me to be faithful to the Lord, come into my house, and abide there." Paul accepted the invitation (Acts 16:15). The converted Philippian jailer brought Paul and Silas into his house and fed them (16:34). On his last trip to Jerusalem, Paul stayed in several homes along the way. He was seven days with disciples at Tyre, one day with brethren at Ptolemais, and many days in the home of Philip the evangelist at Caesarea. Then he took lodging in Jerusalem in the home of an old disciple named Mnason (21:4, 7, 8, 16).

Paul wrote the church of Rome a word of commendation on behalf of Phebe, urging them to receive her and give her assistance. This reception would certainly have included room and board. Paul hints that he had been the recipient of her hospitality (Rom. 16:1, 2).

When Paul wrote the letter to the Romans from Corinth, he acknowledged that at that very moment he was the guest of Gaius. "Gaius, mine host . . . saluteth you" (Rom. 16:23).

Some limitations were placed on entertainment. False teachers were not to receive hospitality, for such lodging was really a form of support. Though ordinary courtesies were not forbidden, no teacher of heresy traveling in his official capacity was to be entertained. Providing hospitality to genuine teachers helped spread truth, but helping false teachers spread error. John wrote, "If there come any unto you, and bring not this doctrine, receive him not into your house, neither bid him God speed: for he that biddeth him God speed is partaker of his evil deeds" (2 John 10, 11). Truth was not to be sacrificed for hospitality or love.

Gaius was commended because he received strangers and helped them forward in their Gospel mission (3 John 5-8). On the other hand, Diotrophes was rebuked because he not only failed to receive the brethen hospitably, but also excommunicated those who wanted to entertain the saints (v. 10).

Instructions, given in the sub-apostolic *Didache* (*Teaching of the Twelve*), written probably between A.D. 80 and 120, labeled as a false prophet any traveling preacher who stayed more than two days or who asked for money for himself. A traveler who wished to settle in a locality was required to work at his craft for his bread. Idleness was considered trafficking on Christ.

One of the most moving examples of Christian hospitality in our century was the hiding of Jews in Europe during Hitler's purge, a kindness jeopardizing the host's life and possessions. *The Hiding Place* by Corrie ten Boom tells of a secret room behind a false wall built in their Holland home. Before detection by German authorities led to her incarceration in a concentration camp, her family hid seven Jews for several months, providing limited but life-saving hospitality.

Blessings
1. The recipient

Certainly the person entertained in another's home receives numerous blessings. More fellow believers than we realize have need for acceptance, fellowship, and love. Single adults, college students, those in the armed forces, families when the mother is away or hospitalized, people in the process of moving, missionaries (and not when just arriving or about to leave) all profit from hospitality. Many couples in metropolitan areas have brought temporal and spiritual help to foreign students who come by the thousands to our shores every year, a veritable mission field wide open to genuine hospitality. It's not magnitude of menu, nor excellence of entertainment that matters but rather the warmth of wantedness and oneness. Not lavish display but a cup of cold water given in Jesus' love will more than suffice. The gift of hospitality provides this kind of fellowship.

The wife of a professor in a college town made it a point to have to their home for an evening all the students enrolled in her husband's classes, eight or ten at a time. Though she did not spread an especially good table, she exuded graciousness. A certain poise about her amidst all the tasks was remarkable. Asked the secret of her ability to entertain with such ease, she replied, "It's all in the way you do it. If it's to impress people, forget it. Your aim should be to appreciate each guest and help in every need."

2. *The host*

No genuinely hospitable person entertains with the hope of getting a return invitation. In fact, Jesus said to invite those who cannot repay (Luke 14:12). Our reward will come from another direction—from above. The motive held out for entertaining strangers, according to the author of Hebrews is, "for thereby some have entertained angels unawares" (13:2). The reference is undoubtedly to the story of Abraham entertaining strangers and discovering them to be angels. Since angels bear God's message and purpose, the entertainment of angels will bring the atmosphere of heaven into the host's home. By extending hospitality to strangers, we may get divine direction and blessing.

Through graciously opening their home to Jesus, Mary and Martha later received the blessing of brother Lazarus' resurrection.

The house of Zaccheus received untold benefit the day he entertained Jesus. "This day is salvation come to this house" (Luke 19:9).

Ananias, when asked to show hospitality to the newly converted Paul, first objected. But what dividends! After Paul received meat, he was strengthened. Not long later Ananias heard Paul preaching Christ in the synagogue (Acts 9:10-20).

When Publius, governor of Melita, received Paul and his shipwrecked partners, lodging them "three days courteously," unanticipated blessing came to Publius in the healing of his seriously ill father through the prayer of Paul (Acts 28:7, 8).

Samuel Rutherford, English theologian, preacher, and one of the composers of the Westminster Confession of Faith, one Saturday evening welcomed a wayfaring stranger into his home. At family worship the stranger betrayed an excellent knowledge of both Bible and catechism. To Rutherford's surprise, the visitor turned out to be the scholarly Archbishop Ussher, primate of the

Church of Ireland who devised the dating known as Ussher's chronology.

Hospitality will pay off in the day of judgment. One determining factor at that time will be whether or not we have offered a welcome to those who need it. "I was a stranger, and ye took Me in" will be words of commendation (Matt. 25:35).

When Dr. Donald C. McKaig, then pastor of Simpson Memorial Christian and Missionary Alliance Church in Nyack, N.Y., gazed down on a hospital bed a few years ago, the patient, whom he had been asked to visit, looked like any other man in the hospital.

Learning that the church was named after Dr. A. B. Simpson, founder of the Christian and Missionary Alliance, the patient volunteered, "When I was a boy, my mother took me to hear Dr. Simpson preach in New York City." He added that his mother had been healed through the prayers of Dr. Simpson.

"Did you ever give your heart to the Lord?" asked McKaig.

"Yes, as a young man I did. But I got away from Him. I've been a backslider for 40 years. The Lord wouldn't have anything to do with me now."

The pastor, assuring him of the Lord's love, was able to lead the patient back to the Lord.

McKaig continued to visit the elderly man. When he left the hospital, McKaig felt sorry for him. The man had no job, scraped along on a small pension, dressed shabbily, drove an old car, and lived in one room in a local boarding house.

The 67-year-old man began to attend Simpson Memorial Church regularly. He made public profession of his renewed faith. Lonely, he would often telephone McKaig for prayer. The pastor, busy as he was, always obliged. Often Pastor and Mrs. McKaig invited him to the parsonage for Sunday dinner.

One day he phoned the pastor, saying, "I want to see you." Thinking he was again down in the dumps, McKaig invited him over. On arrival he informed the pastor, "My brother and I have made out our wills, and we've arranged to leave everything to your church. Whoever dies first will leave all to the surviving brother, and when he passes away, it will all go to the church. We're doing this in memory of our mother."

The man's nearest relatives were 21 first cousins. Then the delightful bombshell burst. "It should amount to at least $100,000."

Four years later the older brother, whom McKaig never met,

died upstate. Days later the surviving brother passed away in the Nyack Hospital. Though none of the 21 first cousins contested the will, legal complications delayed disbursement for over a year. When the will was finally settled, the church learned that it had fallen heir to approximately $125,000.

Simpson Memorial Church, a thriving church today, used the money to build a new sanctuary. It also named a room in memory of the elderly man. Today Cahart Hall is used for board and prayer meetings.

Comments Dr. McKaig, "I've heard about those things happening to others, but never dreamed it would happen to our church." He also knows firsthand the meaning of, "Be not forgetful to entertain strangers; for thereby some have entertained angels unawares" (Heb. 13:2).

13

The Gift
of Giving

A man on a hike came to a steep but short incline. When he lamented that it was too high for him to climb, his companion snatched the protestor's wallet from his pocket and tossed it atop the rise. In a flash the man scrambled up the incline to retrieve his wallet.

A man was about to be baptized in a river. Suddenly he ran back out of the water explaining that he had forgotten to give his wallet to his wife. The preacher called, "Come on back with the wallet. I've got too many unbaptized pocketbooks in my congregation now."

Money is a touchy subject. Someone said that the most sensitive nerve in the human body is the one that leads to the pocketbook. The Bible has much to say about money and stewardship. One of the gifts listed by the Apostle Paul is the gift of giving. "He that giveth, let him do it with simplicity" (Rom. 12:8).

Everybody Is to Give
Throughout this book the point is repeatedly made that absence of a gift does not excuse failure to obey a command in the area of that gift. For example, a person who does not have the gift of evangelism is not exempt from the command to witness. Similarly, a person who does not have the gift of giving is not released from giving. He cannot say, "Great—never again must I put anything on the offering plate, nor give to my church or missionaries." On the contrary, all—with or without the gift of giving—are to give.

In fact, the minimal amount each believer should give is taught in the Bible: the tithe (10%).

Some object to tithing. They claim it is legalistic, comes from Judaism, and was annulled by the cross. Such objectors fall into two categories: those with bad motives and those with good motives. Those with wrong motives oppose tithing because they wish to escape the duty of giving 10% of their income. Free from the law of tithing, they give little or nothing. Their desire to escape the legalism of tithing is just a cover-up for covetousness.

Those who object to tithe-teaching from good motive fear that such instruction may lull people into thinking that when they have given a tenth they have done all God requires in the area of financial stewardship. They are concerned lest emphasis on tithing lead people to selfishly regard the 90% remaining as their own. This dries up the springs of generous giving and undercuts the glorious doctrine of stewardship that views everything we have as God's, not just 10%.

To allay such fears, it should be pointed out that the tithe is a beginning point for giving. If a person under law was required to give 10%, should not those under grace give gladly and gratefully above and beyond the legal tithe?

The claim that tithing is legalistic has its problems, for Abraham and Jacob spoke of the tithe centuries before Moses' law was given. Because the tithe is mentioned from Genesis to Malachi, would not Paul's readers have a pretty good idea of what minimum to give when he wrote, "Upon the first day of the week let every one of you lay by him in store, as God hath prospered him" (1 Cor. 16:2)?

Certainly no one failing to give a tithe to the Lord's work could be considered by any stretch of the imagination to be exercising the gift of giving. In fact, he is really robbing God (Mal. 3:8-10). But on the other hand, the gift of giving involves far more than just tithing.

What Is the Gift of Giving?

Paul says that the gift of giving involves giving "with simplicity" (Rom. 12:8). *Simplicity*, an interesting word, has been translated many ways. Literally, it means *without folds*—as a piece of cloth unfolded—and is rendered *simplicity, singleness of mind, mental honesty, without pretense.* When one gives from such openness of heart, one donates *freely, with delight.* Moreover, he gives *generously, with liberality. Simplicity* in Romans 12:8 has been translated in all of the above ways by one version or another.

The person with the gift of giving will give with singleness of mind. No ulterior motive will ruffle the cloth of his mind to make a fold or two in it. He will not give to salve a conscience uneasy because of the way he acquired his money. Nor will he give to gain something in return. Sending a gift, we might sign "love," but never "I am giving this so that you will admire me." Nor do we give for public show, as did the Pharisees who blew trumpets so people would be alerted to watch them bestow their gifts. The person who will not donate unless his name is inscribed on the stained-glass window or engraved on the cornerstone doesn't understand Christ's command not to let the left hand know what the right hand is doing (Matt. 6:3). The gift of giving permits no alloy of self-seeking in the coin of our gift.

The gift of giving involves giving *freely,* with *delight,* and with love. The January issue of a magazine carried an amusing cartoon. A dirty-looking beggar, extending his hat for a handout, carries a placard which reads, "To give after Christmas—that is true compassion." Real giving is not limited to times and seasons or to a whim of the moment. It reaches from a cheerful heart.

Paul told the Corinthians to give "not grudgingly, or of necessity" (2 Cor. 9:7). The person with the gift of giving will not say, "Oh, if I go to that service they'll take an offering," or, "Here comes the plate; I'll have to put something in, much as it hurts me." The gift of giving does not create a funeral atmosphere at offering time. Rather, one gives cheerfully, "for God loveth a cheerful giver." The Greek word *cheerful* gives us our English *hilarious.* The gift of giving will make offering time a happy occasion, an opportunity to give cheerfully back to Him who has given so much for and to us.

The gift of giving results in *liberality.* One night during a Billy Graham crusade in Madison Square Garden, a well-known underworld character walked in with four bodyguards, who sat two on each side of him. At offering time these men looked to their leader to see what to do. He said, "This is on me, men." Then he pulled from his wallet a roll of $100 bills. (Two members of the Billy Graham team sitting in the row behind reported, "The wad was thick enough to choke a cow.") The underworld character went through these $100 bills till he came to a $1 bill, which he put in the plate.

If this incident were not so lamentable, it would be laughable. The gift was deficient on two major counts. It didn't come from a regenerate heart, and it was not liberal by any stretch of the imagination. The gesture of bare tipping must not be confused with true generosity. Much so-called giving insults God because of its smallness in proportion to capacity to give.

Two Christian lepers in the Orient took a third leper into their hut at a government leprosarium because no official housing was then available. Already the two were existing on a trifle more than starvation rations. When asked how they could possibly feed a third, they replied that though they received rice for two, somehow they would make it do for three. Was not this true liberality?

Another facet of the gift of giving is that *God's work will be helped.* We must not give carelessly and indiscriminately, scattering to every person or group which begs. Rather, by investigation, we will see to it that legitimate needs are met. Donations will not flow in response to emotional or sentimental appeals, nor be granted foolishly, but will be based on careful inquiry.

Summing up, the gift of giving is the God-given ability, perhaps to earn, certainly to give money for the progress of God's work with such care and cheer that the recipients are fortified. God has given some men large possessions because He can trust them to use their assets in divine service. These believers are special stewards. One California pastor remarked that men with money often approach him about financing some ministry at considerable cost to themselves. They derive genuine joy from seeing God work through their gifts. This pastor comments that it's hard to mention a cause without these people wanting to give to it.

This same willing spirit prevailed when poverty continued to rear its head in the Early Church. Property owners sold lands or houses, then donated the proceeds to alleviate need. Barnabas was not only a personification of the gift of encouragement but also the possessor of the gift of giving; he is singled out for special mention as one who sold land and brought the money to the apostles (Acts 4:34-37).

Some men give liberally of their profits, once personal expenses have been met, giving far beyond any tenth.

Present Day Examples

Most American Christians have heard of R. G. LeTourneau, designer and manufacturer of heavy earth-moving equipment. His machinery transformed 5,000 acres of marshland into New York's Idlewild (now Kennedy) Airport, tore open the wilderness for the Alaskan Highway, made airstrips for the landing of the first Allied fighter planes on the beaches of Normandy on D-Day, cleared the debris from bombed-out European cities after World War II.

In the early years of his business, LeTourneau went into partnership with God. By this he did not lower grace to the level of a bargain. Rather he said, "Because I believe that God wants businessmen as well as preachers to be His servants, I believe that a factory can be dedicated to His service as well as a church." In 1935 he irrevocably assigned over 90% of the company's profits to the LeTourneau Foundation, described as a "not-for-profit corporation whose income and capital can be used only for the cause of Christ" (*Moving Heaven and Earth*, Donald Ackland, Iversen-Ford Associates, N.Y., N.Y.).

From the minute LeTourneau made God his business partner, things started to go. In the first 15 years, the Foundation gave over $2.5 million to other organizations engaged in Christian work, and over $2.25 million in its own program of evangelistic ministries. Countless Christian schools and organizations in America have been the recipients of his gift of giving. Scarcely a mission field exists in all five continents where some devoted worker has not been aided through money from this foundation. Altogether, millions of dollars have been given to further the Lord's work.

Power magazine related the story of Albert Archibald who in 1929, with the depression just around the corner, borrowed money to purchase nearly 2,000 acres of seemingly poor land in western Canada. Through foresight and hard work, he developed the land till today it stands among the most valuable farmlands in the Canadian "wheat basket"—Saskatchewan. With the same vision he adopted the amazing personal goal of acquiring and giving away —to Christian organizations—the sum of $1 million.

Through the years he distributed thousands of dollars to a tract organization, thousands more to the Christian and Missionary Alliance, and sizable donations to other missionary societies. One type of work has particularly appealed to Archibald: the Bible training schools and colleges of Western Canada. Chief benefactors have been: Briercrest Bible Institute, Caronport, Saskatchewan; Prairie Bible Institute, Three Hills, Alberta; and Canadian Bible College, Regina, Saskatchewan. To this latter school he has given nearly half a million at crucial periods, making possible its steady growth. About 30 years old, this school has sent over 500 graduates into missionary and ministerial service.

At the time of the *Power* article (September 1971) Archibald, 80, a widower living alone in a modest home, had already given nearly $900,000 to Christian organizations. Certainly he has the gift of giving.

On U. S. 30 outside Lima, Ohio, stands a building 200 feet long. In stainless steel lettering on solid stone, passersby can read, CHRIST IS THE ANSWER. Stanley Tam, founder of States Smelting and Refining Corporation and of a second company, United States Plastic, in early life had an insatiable thirst for making money. Through his conversion and growth in the Christian life, this thirst was transformed into the desire to give money to the Lord's work.

As his business began to prosper, he wanted to make God his Senior Partner. Legal papers were drawn up to turn over 51% of his business to the Lord. Later he upped the amount to 60%, then in 1955 to 100%. The stock in his corporations is not owned by Tam or by any member of his family, but is controlled by Stanita Foundation, a non-profit corporation whose sole purpose is to dispense funds for Christian work around the world. If Tam wanted to regain control of the two firms, he would have to buy back stock from that corporation.

The Foundation gets all sorts of requests for financial aid. The three trustees carefully seek God's guidance and dispense funds to projects they have personally sought out and about which they have asked the Lord's guidance. Tam points out that God is not a blind man with a tin cup. Every believer, whether he has a mite or a million, must seek divine direction in his giving. Stanita Foundation, which some years has received over $250,000, supports more than 20 foreign missionaries, and has a special interest in Christian education of nationals overseas.

The gift of giving is not confined to the rich. Paul spoke of the grace of God bestowed on the churches of Macedonia who gave in the midst of great trial and out of deep poverty to help the poor in Judea (2 Cor. 8:1, 2). The Philippian church, which evidenced

122 / 19 Gifts of the Spirit

the gift of giving by its repeated and solicitous financial help to the Apostle Paul, probably had members of modest or small means. How frequently today people with minimal income want to give to every worthy cause the church undertakes! They show zeal in giving sacrificially.

I sometimes think my parents had the gift of giving. Tithers all their Christian lives, even during depression and unemployment, they gave over and above. As a boy at Christmastime, I well remember my mother walking blocks to deliver money and food to poor families. Also at Christmas they gave personal gifts to many missionaries.

In the summer of 1972, a few weeks before both my father and mother passed away within six weeks of each other, both 89 years of age, they asked me, while on a visit to their home, to do an errand. Unable to attend church since the previous March, they wanted me to deliver their offering envelopes to their local church. On the way I counted an envelope for every one of the 23 Sundays they had missed church. Both were hospitalized six weeks later, and on my return I found six more envelopes all made out for the church.

Folks in charge of a local mission office told me how my father, less than a week before he was hospitalized, blind in one eye and a cataract in the other, stumbled across the main street of a city of 300,000 during rush 5 P.M. traffic to bring his monthly gift. They helped him back across the busy street, wondering how he could make it home.

Just before an ambulance drove up to take my mother to the hospital, barely able to walk and with speech somewhat slurred by a stroke, she told me of a black bank book in a certain drawer, whispering, "That's the Lord's money. Everything in it belongs to Him!"

Giving is a grace that can be cultivated. Perhaps as you advance from victory to victory in the realm of stewardship, you will discover a Spirit-bestowed ability and delight in using temporal possessions for God's glory and man's good.

14

The Gift of Government

A church member, referring to the chairman of the official board, remarked, "That man is the boss of this church. He may not have the title openly but everyone understands his position. He has money. No project goes unless it has his OK. If you want some item to pass, you have to gain his support. He's been board chairman at the church for 20 years and sees to it that he's perpetuated in office. He's the power behind the throne. The pastor does whatever he says. No one dares cross him."

Being such a boss is not good leadership. This modern counterpart of first-century Diotrephes, who loved preeminence and arrogantly asserted his authority over a local church, was not exhibiting the New Testament gift of government (see 3 John 9, 10).

The natural tendency is to want to dominate. This urge to grasp at power was recognized by the Apostle Peter, who advised undershepherds not to act like tyrants over God's flock (1 Peter 5:3).

Bosses—No; Servants—Yes

We hear much today about the two classes: clergy and laity. Is this a legitimate divison? In one sense, it is. To that degree that some people possess the gift of ruling we shall have leaders and people. (Clergy and laity come from Greek words which mean magistrate and people.)

But in the sense of the domineering of people by clergy, this classification is unfortunate and misleading.

Church leaders are not to seek power. When James and John

asked for positions of eminence in the coming kingdom, Jesus replied, "Ye know that they which are accounted to rule over the Gentiles exercise lordship over them; and their great ones exercise authority upon them. But so shall it not be among you; but whosoever will be great among you, shall be your minister; and whosoever of you will be the chiefest, shall be servant of all" (Mark 10:42-44). Unregenerate leadership often involves domination, tyranny, lordship. But Christian leadership is to be characterized by slave-service. The words, *minister* and *servant* in the last verse above, mean *servant* and *slave*.

Jesus Christ gave us a perfect model. He added to the above words, "For even the Son of man came not to be ministered unto, but to minister, and to give His life a ransom for many" (v. 45). He humbled Himself to become a servant, really a slave (Phil. 2:7). After graphically portraying the slave-service of a leader by washing the disciples' feet, He commented, "For I have given you an example, that ye should do as I have done to you. Verily, verily, I say unto you, The servant is not greater than his lord; neither he that is sent greater than he that sent him" (John 13:15, 16).

Significantly, the names of the major offices of the church denote service. The word *deacon* is the word for *minister* or *servant*. *Pastor* is a shepherd, who certainly serves. The title *minister* really means servant. Genuine Christian leadership serves, not bosses. The teaching of the universal priesthood of believers places leader and people on the same level (1 Peter 2:5, 9; Rev. 1:6).

Bosses—No: Leaders—Yes

Despite the universal priesthood of believers which puts all on the same level, despite the lack of biblical backing for domination of laity by clergy, despite the serving-slave characteristic of major church offices, a leadership ministry of some kind is part of the Spirit's gift to the church. Whether paid or volunteer, full-time or part time, leadership gifts do exist.

Christ appointed and trained the Twelve who did some ruling in those very early years of the church (Acts 4:37, 9:27). To supervise the Early Church, the apostles remained in Jerusalem when everybody else scattered abroad (Acts 8:1, 4).

The Twelve advised the election of seven deacons to supervise the distribution of food to the needy, thus freeing the Twelve for concentration on prayer and proclamation. These two groups, the apostles and the deacons, were special. But when we read of Paul's missionary journeys, we soon discover a consistent policy regarding leadership. Sooner or later Paul saw to it that each church had officers. For example, on his return visit to Lystra, Iconium, and Antioch on his first journey, he and Barnabas "ordained them elders in every church" (Acts 14:23). At his first visit when the church was founded, believers would not yet have qualifications for eldership, but by the time of his revisitation some would have matured sufficiently to serve as elders.

Though we do not know when, we do know that elders were appointed at Ephesus (Acts 20:17), and elders (bishops) and deacons at Philippi (Phil. 1:1). Paul left Titus at Crete "that thou shouldest set in order the things that are wanting, and ordain elders in every city, as I had appointed thee" (Titus 1:5). Then Paul listed qualifications for an elder, whom he also termed a bishop (1:6-8). Paul likewise gave Pastor Timothy a list of qualifications for church leaders (1 Tim. 3:1-13), in which he specifically mentions the bishop (elder) taking care of the church of God (v. 5). Paul said that the elder who ruled well should receive double honor, because he does two things: leads as well as teaches (1 Tim. 5:17).

Specifically, though, the gift of ruling, or governments, is mentioned in two of the lists of gifts. In Romans, Paul urges that "he that ruleth" should do it "with diligence" (12:8). In 1 Corinthians, he includes among the gifts—"governments" (12:28). Though the Holy Spirit leads and guides the church, some believers do receive the gift of leadership. The Greek for *bishop* is composed of words which mean "see" and "over"—giving us "overseer" or "superintendent."

The priesthood of believers can be pushed to such extremes that a church may try to operate without leadership. This hampers the work of the Holy Spirit, who gives the gift of ruling. Also, on practical considerations it's difficult to operate without leaders. In actuality, when any church officially has no pastor, it will have an unofficial leader or two.

The New Testament Missionary Fellowship, a New York city group, became the target of a series of abduction attempts. The New York *Times* in a feature article reported that, according to the Fellowship, the members operated along democratic lines, with everyone free to preach or prophesy during meetings, but they also acknowledged that four persons exercised special leadership because of their greater experience. Also, most of the interpretation in tongues-speaking services is done by pastors or leaders. The matter-of-fact, pragmatic operation of church life requires some form of leadership.

Three main words are used with reference to church leadership, two verbs and one noun. The verb *proistemi* means *to stand over, place over, set over, superintend, preside,* and is translated *rule,* when the gift of government is listed in Romans 12:8. The Holy Spirit does place some over others in the church. This verb also refers to a father's rule over his family (1 Tim. 3:5, 12); and to the care officers have of the church (1 Thes. 5:12, 13; 1 Tim. 5:17).

The second word, a noun, *kubernesis,* used of the gift of government in 1 Corinthians 12:28, not only gives us our English *cybernetics,* but also in a closely related form is translated *master* (meaning *helmsman* or *steersman*) in Acts 27:11, and *shipmaster* in Relevation 18:17. The church ship certainly needs captains with the gift of piloting.

The third word, a verb, *hegeomai,* means *to go before, lead, be a leader, rule, command, have authority over.* It is translated *governor* (referring to Joseph over all Egypt in Acts 7:10), *ruler* (Matt. 2:6), and *chief* (Acts 15:22). But it's used for church leadership three times in Hebrews 13. "Remember them which have the rule over you" (v. 7). "Obey them that have the rule over you, and submit yourselves" (v. 17). "Salute all them that have the rule over you" (v. 24).

How Leadership Operates
Christian leadership is never dogmatic, demagogic, nor dictatorial. Rather, spiritual authority expresses itself in wisdom, tact, example, humility, and service.

The seven deacons were chosen because they were "full of the Holy Ghost and wisdom" (Acts 6:3). The gift of wisdom was required to settle tactfully this potentially explosive dispute between ethnic groups in the Jerusalem fellowship.

Scriptural qualifications for church leadership have chiefly to do with exemplariness of life, such as having an above-reproach marriage and sound family rearing, being blameless, soberminded, of controlled temper, self-disciplined, not addicted to wine, not covetous, nor quarrelsome, just, honest, no lover of money— qualities all believers should exhibit. Since such fruitfulness does not mushroom the first weeks of the Christian life, the leader should not be a novice (new plant) lest he fall before pride. Though he does need to be sound in doctrine and to possess the gifts of teaching, ruling, and hospitality, most of the demands relate to a fruitful character (1 Timothy 3:1ff.; Titus 1:5-9). Instead of acting autocratically over God's heritage, he is to be an example to the flock (1 Peter 5:3).

Paul equates leadership with labor. He commands believers, "to know them which labour among you, and are over you in the Lord" (1 Thes. 5:12). In fact, he adds that high esteem is due leaders "for their work's sake" (v. 13). Likewise, the author of Hebrews, in repeating his order to remember and obey spiritual rulers, emphasizes more their service than their authority (13:7, 17). Recall—leaders are not bosses, but servants.

The word *proistamenos,* noun form of "rule" (Rom. 12:8), originally denoted an influential Roman *patron* who had his following or clients. Later the word came to signify any person of wealth and power who exerted himself to help his poor, weak, and uninfluential friends. Clement, about the turn of the first century, applied this word to Christ, whom he called "Guardian of our weakness" (*Epistle of Clement to the Corinthians,* 36:1). Early leadership championed the plight of the poor.

The gift of government runs counter to hierarchical structure. New Testament leadership repudiated pomp, circumstance, and status. Church authority does not deal in terms of office, dignity, eminence, but comes from Christlike example and humble service. That's why a leader's qualifications exclude being overbearing, stubborn, heady, wanting his own way. People who want this gift need the qualifications that go with it. Otherwise, authority not accompanied by spiritual grace breeds anarchy.

The gift of government, then, is the Spirit-given ability to preside, govern, plan, organize, and administer with wisdom, fairness, example, humility, service, confidence, ease, and efficiency.

Areas in Modern Church Life
Someone facetiously suggested that most of the gifts reside in the

pastor and official board, with only one left to the congregations —that of giving to pay the bills.

However, laymen in every congregation should be exercising many gifts, including that of government. Though every official leader of any church should have the gift of ruling, and should not be elected for office involving leadership unless recognized as possessing this gift, yet not all who have this gift will necessarily be elected to an official overseeing position. The gift is exercisable and requisite for many areas of church life outside board officialdom.

Thus, we should expect many in every church to possess it, not only to stock the boards with gifted people but to supply these other needed areas.

Presiding at Meetings

No meeting can really run by itself. The Spirit leads through human instrumentality. Paul's instructions regarding prophecies, tongues, and interpretations in a public meeting require some leader to declare when things are out of order (1 Cor. 14:26-40). Churches that encourage lay participation in testimony, sharing, reading of Scripture, or expressing spiritual truth seem to be growing both in spirituality and size but because of the danger of disorder arising out of congregational excesses, congregations need the firm hand of a leader to see that all things are done decently and in order.

Business meetings need the gift of government. Many a pastor, unversed in the intricacies of Roberts Rules of Order, would warmly welcome the help of some layman-parliamentarian at annual or quarterly business sessions. The day after a church's annual meeting, a member unavoidably absent, meeting another member on the street, received this report: "The meeting went wonderfully smooth. One of our congregation who is an excellent lawyer moderated the business. He moved things right along, graciously brought us back to the discussion at hand whenever we strayed, kept us on the motion, ruled whether or not what we were doing was legal. Oh—it was the best annual meeting the church has ever had!"

Many a church board meeting is presided over, not by the pastor, but by some man whose recognized competence gets him elected chairman.

Handling Discipline

One function of leadership is to prevent disorders through constant vigilance and faithful admonition (1 Thes. 5:12). Or, when the even progress of the body has been upset, to restore harmony. When conflict arose between the youth director and the Sunday School superintendent in a certain church, a special small committee was appointed from the official board to investigate. The gift of ruling was certainly manifested in the wisdom, tact, and meekness of the committee, resulting in the settlement of the dispute to the satisfaction of both parties.

Disciplinary action in the church, excommunication or restoration, is not the prerogative of the pastor. Rather it seems that Paul had the whole church act on such a matter (1 Cor. 5:4). But the mechanics will be handled by duly appointed officers of the church. In discipline matters, the gift of leadership is needed.

Believers are exhorted to obey church leaders, "for they watch for your souls, as they that must give account" (Heb. 13:17).

Boards, Panels, Administration

One pastor hasn't been to a trustee meeting in his church for 15 years because of his implicit faith in the elected officers to efficiently conduct the temporal business of the church. This same pastor attends a bare minimum of other committee meetings, but receives full minutes of every session within days.

Every church, even with minimal organization, has need of various committees other than the official boards, such as evangelism, visitation, music, education, missions. One Pennsylvania church has 22 standing committees. To staff these committees requires dozens of men and women with the gift of government.

Also, literally hundreds of Christian organizations including missionary societies, colleges, seminaries, service organizations, and publishing houses, require the services of executive directors or presidents with the gift of management. This gift, like many others, needs to be sharpened. Dr. John W. Alexander, President of Inter-Varsity, in his book, *Managing Our Work,* says "Management ability is one of the *gifts* of the Holy Spirit. It is also a *science*. There is a body of knowledge and principles (acquired through the experience of our predecessors) to be learned. Further, management is an *art*. There are specific aptitudes and skills to be developed through sustained practice."

Often men leave the pastorate to take over administrative positions in Christian organizations. One middle-aged pastor became a most successful director of development for a Christian college. But without the gift of leadership he would have flopped. Being a good professor of language or science or mathematics doesn't guarantee one will make a competent college president; nor does being a successful preacher portend quality performance as district superintendent.

A healthy sign in evangelicalism today is the springing up of seminars that deal with management, use of time, getting along with fellow workers, putting one's ideas across, and motivation. However, successful completion of a dozen courses can never produce the gift of government, only polish it.

Future Projection
The gift of leadership certainly includes direction for the future. Recall that the word translated *governments* (1 Cor. 12:28) not only gives us our English *cybernetics,* but also is closely allied to *shipmaster* (Acts 27:11; Rev. 18:17). Cybernetics, related to computers, suggests the capacity to make plans according to scriptural programming. *Shipmaster* makes us think of piloting or guiding. We need leaders capable of steering the ship of church safely through rocks and shoals of the future. People with this gift have ability to make plans and launch projects to meet future needs.

In most organizations today, two groups are likely to be found side by side. One group wants to keep on doing things as always, to conduct business as usual; the other strives to reach out to new ways, to attempt something different. One is preserving, the other prophetic. One, conservative, the other creative. One traditional, the other inventive. Perhaps the gift of leadership will know when to stay with the old way of doing things, and also when to innovate with ministries such as coffeehouses, folk-singing concerts, Teen Challenge, Moody Science Films, and L'Abri, the Swiss retreat center for people struggling with doubt and skepticism. Whether piloting the church through unusual or routine maneuvers, the shipmaster must keep the church in balance, lest it stiffen into traditionalism or run riot.

The gift of leadership involves setting goals for the future, motivating people, executing plans, and finally review. Always this must be for ministry to people, not their manipulation. The leader will always be the servant.

No church or church-related organization can exist without leadership. Paul says we should exercise this gift with diligence, responsibility, and zeal (Rom. 12:8).

Then we shall have Christian statesmen.

15

The Gift of Showing Mercy

A terminally ill man became a Christian through the witness of a hospital visitor who brightened every sick room he entered. After listening to the late Dr. Donald Grey Barnhouse on the radio, the new convert expressed a wish to meet the radio preacher. The hospital visitor, a close friend of Dr. Barnhouse, relayed the request. Together the two men went to the hospital. The patient was suffering from advanced cancer which horribly affected one side of his face. As Dr. Barnhouse followed his friend into the room, he was taken back by the smell of death already there. Then his friend laughed gaily, "Hello, John! I've come to see you."

At first, Dr. Barnhouse thought the sick man was unconscious; then he saw a smile break at the corner of his mouth. The friend went down on his knees beside the bed, put his arm under the pillow, and cradled the dying man in his embrace. Smiling, he said, "John, I've been praying for you! I've had assurance that you are being blessed, and that you are going to be with the Lord, full of joy!"

Then he introduced Dr. Barnhouse who later commented, "I tried to talk to the man, but I received much more than I could ever have given. I saw the visitor, through the Holy Spirit, communicate his infectious joy of the Lord, which the sick man needed far more than pious platitudes. As my friend talked, his words flowed with praise to God. He spoke of the wonder of the Lord—how marvelous He is, how He never makes a mistake, how He does all things well, how He would soon take John home to be with Himself, how wonderful it would be to see the Lord Jesus Christ."

Concluded Dr. Barnhouse, "That day I saw the gift of the Holy Spirit in the life of this hospital visitor which enabled him to do such an act of mercy with cheerfulness" (*Commentary on the Epistle to the Romans,* Booklet No. 69, The Evangelical Foundation, Philadelphia, Pa.).

The gift of showing mercy is the Spirit-guided ability to manifest practical, compassionate, cheerful love toward suffering members of the body of Christ. Paul included the gift in his Romans list: "He that showeth mercy, with cheerfulness" (12:8).

Feels Pity

The verb *show mercy* may be translated *to pity, commiserate, have compassion on, show gracious favor to.* When disaster strikes, people invariably feel pity. But too often, this emotion soon dies to wait the next report of tragedy.

But the pity involved in this gift is not just the stirring of the emotions, but deep-down compassion, supernatural in origin. It's not just kindness springing from man's heart, but is divine love, under the Spirit's guidance, acting in Christ's name, with the object of glorifying the Father.

Whoever has this gift does not steel himself in the face of another's miseries. Rather he is drawn to his suffering brother. He must do something about it. The gift involves more than a feeling of pity; it requires action.

Involves Deeds

When seven members of a Chicago family died because of leaking gas fumes, a grief-stricken mother was left with an enormous bill for hospitals, funerals, and cemetery plots. A little church started a collection which snowballed to the neighboring community. But one man sent in an envelope with nothing in it but a poorly printed tract entitled, "How to Be Saved." He hadn't learned that real mercy demands more than words.

Whenever Jesus was moved with compassion, He did something about it. His pity, no vague abstraction, was expressed in concrete deeds of mercy. He healed the blind, the lepers, the sick. He fed the multitudes. His whole life on earth demonstrated His compassion. His sacrifice on the cross was the supreme evidence of this pity.

The same word used for the gift in Romans 12:8 appears several times in the Gospels when people cried, "Have mercy on me," as in the case of the two blind men, a mother on behalf of her demon-possessed daughter, a father for his demon-possessed son, Bartimaeus, and 10 lepers. They wanted performance, not just pity. And Jesus did something in each case.

In a New England village a home burned. Some furniture was saved and four cows, but not much else. The victims needed almost everything. A neighbor drove up to gawk at the smoking ruins and to poke around the scorched shell. Shaking his head as though in unbelief and clearing his throat, he told the owner, his long-time neighbor, "If there's anything I can do, just say the word." Then he drove away, leaving behind his "ritual words." Other neighbors came too, but instead of asking what they could do, for one would have to be blind not to see, they returned with help: beds, mattresses, potatoes, vegetables, cooking pots, clothes, hay for the cows. For the person who possesses the gift of showing mercy, "How can I help?" is not just a proper phrase, offered merely for the record to take care of one's conscience, but a mean-business question leading to taking care of the person in need.

As James put it, "If a brother or sister be naked, and destitute of daily food, and one of you say unto them, Depart in peace, be ye warmed and filled; notwithstanding ye give them not those things which are needful to the body; what doth it profit?" (James 2:15, 16) The gift of showing mercy doesn't end with only caring, but with sharing.

Of course, it's possible to speak genuine words of encouragement. Speaking words of strength in a sick home evidences the gift of exhortation, but going into the kitchen to cook a meal displays the gift of mercy.

Early believers showed mercy by selling lands and houses to help the poor among them (Acts 2:44, 45).

Dorcas, whom Peter raised from the dead at Joppa, was much beloved for her sanctified needlework which made coats and other garments for poor widows. She is described as "full of good works and almsdeeds which she did" (Acts 9:36). *Almsdeeds* could be translated *mercy-deeds*. Dorcas, indeed, had the gift of showing mercy.

The newly converted Philippian jailor showed mercy within a few minutes of his conversion. He washed the stripes on the backs of Paul and Silas, coated with coagulated blood, brought them into his house, and fed them (Acts 16:33, 34).

A graphic example of this gift is found in Onesiphorus. On a trip to Rome, he diligently sought out Paul, who then was a prisoner, not in his own hired house but likely in some dank, dark, dungeon-like jail, perhaps the Mamertine prison. Though imprisonment was severe, all access to the outside world was not barred. Paul seems to imply that fear of persecution or the shame of association with him kept Christians at Rome from helping as much as they should have. But Onesiphorus "oft refreshed me, and was not ashamed of my chain: But, when he was in Rome, he sought me out very diligently, and found me" (2 Tim. 1:16, 17). Think of poor Paul whose expansive spirit liked to roam the world, now chained. Think of this gregarious man with a host of friends and no one coming to see him—except Onesiphorus whose name literally means "help-bringer" or in broader terms "mercy-doer."

This gift will enable its possessor to decide whether to help directly or indirectly. Sometimes it may be more merciful not to give a person a direct handout. One might give a man work to do or show a woman how to sew or manage a household. This gift will enable a Christian nurse to know when to stop feeding the seriously injured automobile accident victim and when to stop helping him walk down the hallway, and mercifully make him learn to take care of himself.

Requires Cheerfulness

A well-known evangelist spent two weeks in bed with pneumonia. Ministerial acquaintances came from a distance, and despite his high fever, spent over an hour in the sick room, exuding oppressive melancholy. They left with the reminder that, if they never met on earth again, they would certainly meet in glory. The evangelist reported, "I was far sicker when they left than when they came."

So often we show mercy from a sense of duty, or with a scowl, or grudgingly, "I'll help you this time, but . . ."

A church member who wanted to help in some form of Christian activity was assigned the task of standing outside a rescue mission, inviting people to enter. He did so in a very mournful manner. Each passerby glanced at him and went on. He learned his lesson when one man responded to his gloomy invitation, "No thanks, I've troubles enough of my own."

A little girl said of a pious deacon, "He must be a very good man; he always looks so sad."

Paul specifically states that this gift must be exercised with cheerfulness (Rom. 12:8). The visitor to sick and shut-in people must radiate sunshine. Not like the man visiting his incurably ill wife, who held up the deed to their cemetery lots and said, "All's well. Don't fret."

Those who are versed in the Talmud tell us that halfhearted or grudging almsgiving to the poor is without merit. Not how much but how well one serves means more in the sight of God. Also, children who provide for their parents with finest foods and lavish luxuries, but with ill grace, incur divine displeasure.

Doing mercy with a growl nullifies the service. The gift of showing mercy, through the inner stimulus of the Holy Spirit, makes the doer of mercy a veritable sunbeam, penetrating the sick chamber to the very heart of the afflicted.

When Madame Guyon, French mystic, was jailed in the Bastille in 1699, her devout maidservant chose to share her mistress' imprisonment. She believed her mistress could never survive the dread incarceration alone and would need a constant attendant to minister to her. This she did cheerfully till her own death in 1700, just before Madame Guyon was released.

Strengthens Many

The extent to which this gift can bring comfort to the suffering members of the body of Christ is virtually unlimited because of the vast, diverse, heart-rending needs of God's people. Though believers must extend mercy to unbelievers, the purpose of gifts is the edification of God's people. We are to do good to all men, but especially to the household of faith (Gal. 6:10). Primarily, this gift is exercised toward suffering saints.

How does the gift of mercy differ from the gift of helps? The gift of helps is directed toward Christian workers to release them from temporal service so they can concentrate on their primary ministry of the Word and prayer. The gift of mercy is directed toward the saint in distress, the outcast, the poor, the underprivileged, the ill, the deprived, the handicapped, the retarded, the unlovely, the shut-in, the hungry, the alcoholic.

Nursing homes and old people's infirmaries are full of people once active in evangelical churches. They pass away the lonely months, longing for someone to bring a little sunshine. One church ladies group sponsors a birthday party each month for old folks in their local home.

A widow due back from a two-month hospital stay found her house spick and span, cleaned from top to bottom by young ladies from her church.

How often hot evening meals brought into a home where the mother is hospitalized have strengthened the distressed family.

When a church member's house was badly burned, other members rallied around, devoting long evening and Saturday hours to erecting a temporary but suitable shelter where the family could live till their original house was restored.

We are to contribute to the needs of God's people (Rom. 12:13; Heb. 13:16). In fact, the ex-thief is told to get an honorable occupation so that he will have something to give to the needy (Eph. 4:28). We are to comfort the feebleminded and to support the weak (1 Thes. 5:14). Some people need to get anchored emotionally. People need mercy as well as medicine. Where needed and possible, children are to give some financial support to their parents (1 Tim. 5:4). Some translators speak of children repaying parents for all the good the latter have bestowed on their offspring. Exercising mercy includes being impartial to outsiders and kind to minority groups. For some, it may mean a ministry in the inner city. Mercy deeds do not have to be known for their magnitude. Jesus said, "Whosoever shall give you a cup of water to drink in My name, because ye belong to Christ, verily I say unto you, he shall not lose his reward" (Mark 9:41).

The Boy Scout slogan about doing a good deed for the day is not such a bad idea. Despite the belittling of works in some circles, the Bible is strong on good works as the evidence of faith and love.

In our day of ease, when softness, convenience, and apathy prevail in much of the church, we might be stirred to the doing of deeds of mercy by a reminder from the life of John Wesley, when he was 82 years of age. "At this season [New Year] we usually distribute coal and bread among the poor of the Society. But I now considered, they wanted clothes as well as food. So on this day and the four following days I walked through the town and begged 200 pounds in order to clothe them that needed it most. But it was hard work as most of the streets were filled with melting snow, which often lay ankle-deep; so that my feet were steeped in snow water nearly morning till evening. I held out pretty well till Saturday evening; but I was laid up with a violent flux, which increased every hour till, at 6 in the morning, Dr. Whitehead called upon me" (*Journal*, Jan. 4, 1785).

In Jacksonville, Fla., the Dinsmore Baptist Church carries on an unusual ministry to 45 handicapped folks. It was started in 1969 by Pastor J. W. Wynn after several visits to a young man left paralyzed from the neck down by an auto accident. The Dinsmore Club, as it is called, sends out two buses to pick up club members for weekly four-and-a-half hour Tuesday meetings. Equipped with hydraulic lifts for easy handling of the wheelchairs in which most club members must be transported, these buses travel as far as 50 miles away to pick up and return their riders. Though not a rehabilitation program, the club has improved the physical condition of many. One whose handicap made him doubt the worth of living found strength and purpose by teaching another how to put a spoon of food in his mouth for the first time in eight years. Tears of joy flowed that day. Over and over, hearts are softened because of the Christlike love members have for each other.

Our deeds of mercy may be the strongest witness to the outside world of our faith in Christ. A professor of political science at Miami University in Oxford, Ohio, recently wrote, "The most important contribution almost all of us make in this world is in our interpersonal relations. Our personal acts of kindness and concern have probably a hundred times more actual impact on the lives of others than our advocacy of 'enlightened' social ideas.

"College professors, for instance, may talk endlessly and learnedly about social reforms. Yet for all but a very, very few, I believe the only part of their lives that really makes much difference to the real lives of others is the way they treat their wives or husbands, their children, their neighbors, their students in and out of class—and the general moral example they set. The world would probably not be one whit the worse if 95 percent of all the books and learned articles were never written and most of the lectures never delivered. But each time an individual performs an act of kindness, someone's life is brightened at least a little. Wordsworth wisely spoke of 'that best part of a man's life, his little nameless, unremembered acts of kindness and of love.'

"If the principal impact of almost all political activists is found

not in their political ideas and activities but in their personal relations, then should not the churches largely concentrate on helping all of us make the most of our private lives and relationships?
This is where the action really is; this is the crucial battle ground
for 98 percent of us 98 percent of the time" ("The Church and
Public Policy," Reo M. Christenson copyright 1973 by *Christianity
Today*.)

During the Italian occupation of Ethiopia, evangelicals suffered
severe persecution. Since the jails made no provision for feeding
prisoners, the only way they ate was for relatives and friends to
bring food. Christian prisoners were so well cared for by fellow
believers and church groups that extra food was passed on to non-
Christian prisoners, often forgotten by relatives and friends. This
spontaneous, unspoken witness of deep love, unheard of in non-
Christian circles, caused unbelievers to seek out Christians to
learn more of this new way. Also, as a result, many prisoners
who accepted Christ, when released, went home to seek out the
nearest evangelical church.

Today every child of God needs to manifest practical, compassionate love to other members of the body of Christ. Those
who have the gift of showing mercy should especially be about
this greatly needed ministry.

16

The Gift
of Faith

In 1973 a church on Route 46 in Netcong, N.J., faced an insurmountable problem. They had just built a new sanctuary on their recently acquired eight-acre property, half of which was mountain and woods. They were told they would not be granted permanent occupancy until they had sufficient parking in the rear. The trouble was, 40 feet of sheer mountain rose abruptly at the back of the church, leaving insufficient space for the legally required parking lots. The cost to remove the mountain was prohibitive for the church. One Sunday morning Pastor Ray Crawford reminded the congregation of Christ's promise, "If ye have faith as a grain of mustard seed, ye shall say unto this mountain, Remove hence to yonder place; and it shall remove; and nothing shall be impossible unto you" (Matt. 17:20). Then he added, "If you believe that, come on Wednesday night to pray with me that God will move this mountain from the back of our church."

Next morning the phone rang. It was the telephone company. They were planning to erect a new building and needed fill for a large swampy site. They had learned that the mountain back of the church had the correct proportions of sand, clay, and rock for the required fill. Within a month the phone company hauled away 40,000 square yards of fill, for which they paid the church $5,400, not only removing the mountain but leveling the ground for the required three parking lots and preparing them for paving.

The gift of faith, listed by Paul in 1 Corinthians 12:9, is *more* than saving faith. No one can enter the Christian life without exercising genuine faith. "For by grace are ye saved through faith" (Eph. 2:8). To continue the Christian life also requires faith. "For we walk by faith, not by sight" (2 Cor. 5:7). However, not all believers possess the faith to remove mountains. The inclusion of mountain-moving faith in the list of gifts distinguishes it from saving faith (1 Cor. 13:2).

The gift of faith is a Spirit-given ability to see something that God wants done and to sustain unwavering confidence that God will do it regardless of seemingly insurmountable obstacles. Stephen, full of faith, was enabled to perform miracles (Acts 6:8). One wonders if, at his defense before the Sanhedrin and then at his stoning, Stephen may have picked out ringleader Saul and claimed him for salvation with the gift of faith.

Making the Impossible Possible
A blind man with the gift of faith, when asked by the Lord to make his request, would never say, "Please, Lord, give me a white cane." He would ask for the impossible—sight.

Though all logic seems stacked against some course of action, this faith makes decisions which seem senseless, then sees them through despite overriding objections and massive roadblocks. This gift sees the will of God accomplished despite all natural resistance. Specializing in the impossible—"rivers that are uncrossable and mountains you can't tunnel through"—the gift of faith "laughs at impossibilities and cries, 'It shall be done.' "

Almost every book that discusses the gift of faith refers to the life and ministry of George Müller, who by faith operated an orphanage in Bristol, England. He cared for 10,000 orphans over a period of 60 years, receiving $5 million in the process. He began the work with only two shillings in his pocket. Without once making known any need, he received enough to build five large homes, able to house 2,000 orphans, and to feed the children day by day, all by faith and prayer. Never did they go without a meal. Often the pantry was bare when the children sat down to eat, but help always arrived in the nick of time.

One morning when not a speck of food or milk was on hand to feed the hundreds of hungry orphans seated expectantly at the breakfast table, Mr. Müller prayed, "Father, we thank Thee for the food Thou art going to give us."

Came a knock at the door. A baker stood there. "I was awakened at 2 A.M. and felt I should bake some bread for you."

A few minutes later came another knock. A milkman said, "My milk wagon just broke down in front of your place. I must get rid of these cans of milk before I can take the wagon for repairs. Can you use this milk?" Müller testified that thousands of times they were without food for another meal and without funds, but not once did God fail to provide food.

Strict rules governed the acceptance of gifts. No appeals whatsoever were made. Never was any existing need revealed to any outsider, lest it be construed as a request for aid. Müller once withheld an annual report to keep people from knowing the orphanage's dire financial straits. Though he never asked for money, he did ask for more orphans. Nor would he accept money from those in debt, once returning such a gift, even though insufficient funds were on hand to meet the expenses of the day.

Believing That God Wants It

The possessor of this gift will limit his asking to only those things God wants. His desire will correspond with God's desire. Faith is firm conviction that God wishes to do something remarkable. Faith thinks big—but thinks the kind of big God wants.

Müller always first satisfied himself that he was doing God's will before he started a project. Then, resting on the promises of the Bible, he came boldly to the throne in prayer, pleading his case argumentatively, giving reasons why God should answer. No delay discouraged him. Once he was persuaded that a thing was right, he went on praying for it till the answer came. He said, "I never give up! Tens of thousands of times have my prayers been answered!" A stickler for details, he kept a complete record of prayers; it covered 3,000 pages, contained nearly a million words, and chronicled over 50,000 specific answers.

Thanking in Advance—Announcing It Will Be So

The gift of faith prompts prayer like that of Jesus when He raised Lazarus. Jesus thanked the Father in advance, as though the answer were an accomplished fact. "Father, I thank Thee that Thou hast heard Me. And I knew that Thou hearest Me always; but because of the people which stand by I said it, that they may believe that Thou hast sent Me" (John 11:41, 42).

A trans-Atlantic sea captain, after 22 hours on the ship's bridge in a dense fog off the banks of Newfoundland, was startled by a tap on the shoulder. It was Müller, then in his 70s. "Captain, I have come to tell you I must be in Quebec on Saturday afternoon." This was Wednesday.

When the captain said it was impossible, Müller replied, "If your boat can't take me, God will find some other way. I've never broken an engagement in 57 years."

"I'd like to help," responded the captain, "but what can I do?"

"Let's go below and pray," Müller suggested.

"But Mr. Müller, don't you know how dense the fog is?"

"My eye is not on the fog, but on God who controls the fog and every circumstance of my life."

Down on his knees, Müller prayed the simplest prayer the captain had ever heard. In his opinion it fit a child of nine. "O Lord, if Thou wilt, remove this fog in five minutes. Thou dost know the engagement made for me in Quebec for Saturday."

Putting his hand on the captain's shoulder, Müller restrained him from praying. "First, you don't believe God will do it, and second, I believe He has done it, so there's no need for you to pray. Open the door, Captain, and you'll find the fog gone." And so it was. Müller kept his Saturday engagement in Quebec.

Modestly, Müller wrote, "It pleased the Lord to give me in some cases something like the gift of faith, so that unconditionally I could ask and look for an answer."

The day after Memorial Day in 1939 the *Courier-Express* of Buffalo, N.Y., carried this headline, "Worker of Modern Miracles Dies at 80." It told of the passing of Mrs. Abigail Townsend Luffe, known as "Sister Abigail," founder of El Nathan Home for invalids and aged women. Over her picture appeared in bold type, "She Had Faith." For 38 years, telling her needs to no one but by prayer to God, she cared for dozens of shut-in and elderly ladies. The large amounts of food required plus the helping hands to nurse all came through prayer. In addition, the cost of her $26,000 home was paid in less than six years, quite an accomplishment for a lady who began her work with a single $1 bill.

The gift of faith was evident in her life in other ways as well. One day when she was scheduled to go to New York City to speak at a church service, she lacked $2 of the train fare. Taking her suitcase, she boarded a streetcar for the railroad depot. Suddenly she felt her suitcase lifted by someone with a strong arm helping her into the streetcar. "I'll carry your suitcase, mother," said a soldier. "Where are you going?"

"To New York," answered surprised Sister Abigail.

"So am I. We'll go together."

In the station he led her to a seat, saying, "I'll get the tickets."

Suddenly recalling that she was $2 short, she prayed that she would not be shamed before this stranger by having to tell him she didn't have enough money. Feeling that perhaps she had counted wrong, or that God would somehow multiply the bills in her pocketbook, she started to open it. Suddenly the soldier's big hand came down over hers and shut her purse. "This is my treat, mother," he said.

As they boarded the train, he steered her to an empty coach. She was about to ask him why he bought her ticket when 50 more soldiers pushed into the coach, saluting the officer with her. Taking her gently by the hand, he drew her to her feet, saying, "Boys, I want you to meet my mother."

They looked puzzled, but no more than Sister Abigail. "She's my spiritual mother!" he explained. "She led me to accept Christ during Billy Sunday's meetings in Buffalo a few years ago."

Sister Abigail was delighted to see the fruit of her witness. But even better, as the train puffed out of the station, the officer who had bought her ticket said, "This outfit's on its way to France. Many are not Christians. Will you talk to them?" And for 15 minutes Sister Abigail preached the Gospel.

Turns Vision Into Reality

The gift of faith is often related to the gift of government, which grants prophetic leadership for the planning of future programs. The gift of faith goes beyond envisioning something that God wants done. It believes that it will be realized despite its unlikeliness, then launches out to accomplish the project in God's name. Barnabas, sent by the apostles to investigate the reports of Gentile faith up at Antioch and seeing the genuineness of their profession, captured in his imagination the dream of a magnificent church (Acts 11:23, 24). With the gift of faith he claimed a great work, sought the assistance of Paul, and watched it grow into an influential, missionary-sending church, base of operations for all of Paul's missionary journeys. Through faith, the potential becomes the actual, giving substance to William Carey's motto, "Attempt great things for God—expect great things from God."

Men who started the faith missionary societies, the Bible schools and Christian colleges, and many other evangelical ministries, likely had the gift of faith. Hudson Taylor, founder of the China Inland Mission, sent out an urgent appeal in 1875 that God would raise up 18 suitable workers that year. By the end of the year 18 new workers came. At Christmas 1877 he asked friends to pray for at least 30 new workers the next year. By the end of next December, 28 new workers had sailed, with several others accepted by the mission and scheduled to follow shortly.

In 1881 he estimated a need of 50 or 60 new missionaries in the immediate future. Remembering the Lord had appointed 70, he called a special prayer meeting to petition the Lord for 70 new workers in the next three years. After two years 46 more were needed to complete the 70. Before the third year was up, another 46 sailed.

In 1887 news reached England that Hudson Taylor was fervently praying for 100 new missionaries. He said with the gift of faith, "If you showed me a photograph of the whole 100 taken in China, I could not be more sure than I am now." Before the year ended, more than 600 offered themselves for service. After careful evaluation, 102 were finally selected, all sailing by December 29.

Knows When Helpless Situation Is Not Hopeless

In recent years Corrie ten Boom has become well known as the lady who saw God work in wondrous ways during World War II. First, as a Hollander, she and her family saved the lives of many Jews during Hitler's purge. Then arrested and incarcerated in Ravensbruck concentration camp, she experienced thrilling answers to prayer and miraculous protection. After the war she started a home for the needy back in Holland. Now 80 years of age and very active, her life from age 50 has been filled with incident after incident proving that the gift of faith makes helpless situations not hopeless.

After the war she knew God wanted her to go to the United States to relate her experiences. With $50 in her purse, the maximum permitted by her government, and two borrowed blank checks, she landed among the skyscrapers of New York City. Before she left Holland, relatives aware of her plans shook their heads in disbelief, warning of difficulty in making one's way in

America. Corrie replied that she believed them, but that since God was directing her, she had to obey.

After staying a week in the New York YMCA, Corrie was informed by the clerk that due to demand for rooms she could stay no longer. Corrie replied that the Lord had another room for her, though she did not know the address. The clerk looked puzzled, then suddenly recalled that a letter had arrived for Corrie. Reading the letter, Corrie told the clerk to send her suitcases to a certain address on 109th Street. When the clerk asked why she hadn't known before where to send them, Corrie replied that she got the address from the letter. A woman who had heard Corrie speak that week had written to offer her son's room while he was in Europe. The clerk at the desk was amazed.

Arriving at the address, Corrie found a large house occupied by many families. She found the right apartment at the end of a hall, but no one was home. Arranging herself among her suitcases, Corrie fell asleep to be found by her hostess after midnight. She was a guest for five weeks.

During those five weeks her faith was tested. One check had now been cashed. Looking up addresses given her before she left Holland, she found Americans friendly, interested in her story, but unable to arrange meetings at present. Some curtly suggested she should have stayed in Holland. Her reply was always that God had directed her and that she had a message of His keeping power in a concentration camp.

Finally, her money was all gone. She had cashed the second and last check, and whatever little money she had in Holland she could not get over to America. She prayed. A load lifted as she was sure that though the situation seemed hopeless, God would see her through. Two days later without money, and with no one wanting to hear her story, she attended a Dutch service. When she introduced herself to the speaker, her name revived a memory. He had heard of a woman by that name who experienced miracles in a concentration camp and wondered if she were related to that woman. When Corrie responded that she was that woman, he invited her to speak to his Staten Island congregation and to spend several days with his family. The meals were delightful, quite a change from 25¢ breakfasts of orange juice, two doughnuts, and coffee, while standing at a counter.

Attending a church on Easter Sunday, she met the editor of a

Christian magazine, who gave her an address in Washington, D.C. Corrie wondered if she was getting the runaround as she had so many times, but she traveled to the capital. A dinner in a home led to addressing a women's group. One of the women gave Corrie a check, just enough to cover the amount she had borrowed through the two blank checks.

Then, the tables turned. Instead of no meetings and no work, she now had to guard against overwork as for 10 months she ministered across America, in cities, towns, churches, prisons, colleges, and clubs. Then God led her to Germany, one land where she didn't want to go. But again, the gift of faith saw her through.

Does the "Impossible"

Camp Hope, 55 miles north of New York City on a 220-acre site, is probably the first camp in the world trying to show multiple handicapped and retarded children how to enjoy the life of faith in Christ. Founder and director of the camp, Rev. Winfield Ruelke, affectionately known as Uncle Win, says he started the camp when a lady, a total stranger, asked him one day in 1951, "Is anybody trying to reach the souls of handicapped children in the New York area?" Already having launched a Sunday School for physically handicapped children in the city, Ruelke determined to give these children the advantage of camp experience. He was strongly advised against it by doctors, hospital officials, and church leaders. But convinced the Lord wanted this, Ruelke pioneered through problems experts said were insurmountable. The number of campers grew till 180 different young people spend three weeks at Camp Hope each summer.

Practically all the facilities for this camp came as a result of prayer. Ruelke has been the recipient of such amazing answers that people have likened him to a modern George Müller. He can recite an endless stream of incidents. For example, when he started his camp, he realized the need of special beds. A phone call came from a New York City hospital administrator, "I just told the maintenance crew to get rid of some beds in our basement. Do you need any?" Ruelke had been thinking of starting with 12 campers. When the truck brought the old hospital beds, Ruelke found 12 good beds and a broken one which could be repaired.

When fluorescent lights were needed for a dormitory, Ruelke prayed. A man, totally unaware of the problem, phoned, "We're taking some lights out of our office. Can you use them?" Just when lights were needed for later buildings, the same man phoned again with similar offers.

When Ruelke started an all-year-round resident elementary school for the handicapped and children with problems in 1960, he decided to have a short conference for senior youth who had been to Camp Hope in earlier years. As yet, the building had little furniture and no beds for the 20 young people who had signed up in advance. Opening afternoon came. Bed time was scheduled for 10 P.M. At 6 P.M. someone knocked on the door. "A motel down the road is closing. We purchased some beds. If you can use them, we'd like to give them to you. We have them with us." There were 20 beds and 20 mattresses.

Who Has the Gift?

The gift of faith cannot be demanded, for like all gifts, it is Spirit-bestowed as the Spirit wills. Also, the gift must be used, not boastfully, but lovingly, for though one has mountain-moving faith but not love, he is nothing (1 Cor. 13:2).

Learning of others who have had the gift may cause a person to examine himself to see if he has it too. Müller's example inspired many other faith works. On his world tour, he visited two orphanages—one in Holland, the other in Japan—both started by men who received their impetus through hearing of his work. Müller's experiences encouraged Hudson Taylor to launch the China Inland Mission on a faith principle. The founders of a children's home in Pennsylvania derived the idea for their faith venture from a visit to Müller's institution. Sister Abigail, mentioned earlier as the founder of El Nathan Home in Buffalo, spent many of her childhood hours in Müller's presence observing him exercise the gift of faith, for her father and Müller were close friends. In fact, one biographer suggests that practically every faith work since George Müller's time may be traced directly or indirectly to him.

Even if we don't have the gift of faith, we are commanded to have faith. Several times our Lord rebuked His disciples because of their little faith. Perhaps we should seek more opportunities to develop our faith. A nine-year-old girl made a faith-pledge of 25¢ a week to the missionary giving of her church, a large amount since she had no allowance. Through odd jobs for her mother or

neighbors, she always managed to have the quarter for her offering envelope each Sunday.

But one Saturday night, she didn't have a cent. It was too late
to earn the money. She thought she might borrow it from her
mother, then earn enough to pay it back next week. But then she
decided to pray. "Dear Lord, You've seen me through every week
for 6 months. Please I'd like to give You a quarter tomorrow for
Your missionaries."

Her mother told her to get her clothes ready for Sunday School.
She got out her dress, shoes, and purse. Her mother, seeing her
purse, remarked, "It doesn't match your shoes. Better use your
other purse." Moments later the little girl came running all excited,
"Mother, there's something in it. Hear it jingle." Opening the
other purse, the excited little girl found a quarter she somehow
had left there by mistake. When that girl grew up and attended
Bible college, her faith-training stood her in good stead. Because
her parents had little money, she had to trust the Lord time and
time again to supply her needs.

Do we need to say, "Lord, increase our faith"?

17

The Gift
of Discernment

When a family moved to another state, a major disappointment was leaving the church where they had worshiped for 10 years. Their pastor exhorted them to join a Gospel preaching church in their new community. The family tried two churches. The first certainly honored Christ, but it was a shabby store-front affair whose members appeared low on the social scale. The family wondered if they might find a place of worship with middle-class members where their children might know some friends from their neighborhood.

Not far from their residence they discovered a large church with an impressive sanctuary and affluent members. Many of their children's friends attended Sunday School there. On their first Sunday, Easter, the sermon dealt with the risen Christ and His presence with people today. They visited a few more Sundays, hearing references to the divine Christ and the inspired Bible. A month later they joined.

About three months later a feeling of uneasiness enveloped the parents when their children brought home the news from Sunday School that the way Jesus fed the 5,000 was by getting the lad with the loaves and fishes to bring out his lunch, thus encouraging everyone else to take out his dinner bag. The parents listened more intently to the sermons, but the language seemed so sound. It took them another nine months to discover that, when the preacher spoke of the risen Christ, he meant that only His influence had emerged from the tomb, not His body; when he spoke of an inspired Bible, he meant that the Bible was inspired like the writings of Shakespeare, but not infallible.

The family withdrew to join the store-front church which now was planning to erect a modern sanctuary. Their children found friends from their street in this Sunday School. But that family lost one year of spiritual growth because they lacked discernment.

During a community crusade an evangelist told his life story in which he related such impressive incidents that one pastor, whose avocation was writing, thought he would submit an article on the evangelist for some Christian periodical. In an interview which he gave reluctantly, the evangelist made several more impressive claims, such as holding degrees from certain schools, having sung at the Metropolitan Opera, having worked for the CIA, and having been a prisoner of war.

Excited at the spectacular nature of the story, the pastor related some of the outstanding incidents to a friend in the next town. Listening calmly, the friend quietly suggested the pastor do a little checking on his facts. On investigation the pastor was amazed to discover that not one of the evangelist's claims could be verified. Confronted weeks later with his deception, the evangelist broke down and admitted his lies. That pastor's friend had discernment. The pastor, who admitted he had been "taken," lacked it.

Need for Discernment

A major conflict is being waged between God and His forces, and Satan and his cohorts. Satan doesn't always oppose God directly but often tries to impede by counterfeit. "Satan himself is transformed into an angel of light. Therefore it is no great thing if his ministers also be transformed as the ministers of righteousness" (2 Cor. 11:14, 15). The Satanic counterfeiter makes these imitations:

For Christ there is Antichrist.

For true prophets there are false prophets.

For true apostles there are false apostles.

For wheat there are tares.

For sheep there are wolves in sheep's clothing.

For the Holy Spirit and holy angels there are unclean spirits.

How do we tell the genuine from the spurious? For this we need discernment.

The Bible clearly teaches the existence of a spirit world. Demons are spirit beings, without body, invisible, intelligent, strong (a demon-possessed Gadarene was able to break chains), depraved, fallen, some imprisoned, some free, doomed, opponents of God, and oppressors of man.

Sadly, the non-Christian world seems to have more belief in the spirit world than do some segments of the church. In the United States, 10,000 full-time, and 175,000 part-time astrologers ply their trade. Two-thirds of our newspapers have astrology columns. Though no university offers any course in astrology as a bona fide science, some colleges have added courses to study the phenomena of the occult. Forty million Americans dabble in it. Six thousand spiritist meetings exist across the country. The First Satanic church of San Francisco has more than 10,000 members "with a demon in each man." A quarter-million Satanic Bibles are on the market. Witchcraft is widely practiced. Other doings related to the spirit world today include séances, levitations, apports, telekinesis, visions, automatic writing, trance-speaking, materializations, apparitions, card-laying, psychometry, palmistry, divining with rods, black magic, white magic, and mesmerism.

Though the Christian is forbidden by God's Word to traffic in any way in spiritism (Deut. 18:10-14), he may have to confront false religion promoted by seducing spirits. Such false teachings Paul dubs "doctrines of devils" (1 Tim. 4:1). Lying spirits, whose aim is to deceive are mentioned in the Old Testament. Paul sums it up, "We wrestle not against flesh and blood, but against principalities, against powers, against the rulers of darkness of this world, against spiritual wickedness in high places" (Eph. 6:12).

When a Christian is faced with the supernatural, he is not to mistakenly identify the supernatural with the divine and thus uncritically accept all spirits. Nor is he to be overcritical lest he despise prophesying and quench the Spirit (1 Thes. 5:19, 20). The late Dr. Will H. Houghton, when president of Moody Bible Institute, was approached by a woman who was linked with a false cult which claimed inspiration from the spirit world. When he said he couldn't go along with her belief, she replied that he should trust the spirits. Suddenly this verse came to Dr. Houghton's mind: "Beloved, believe not every spirit, but try the spirits whether they are of God: because many false prophets are gone out into the world" (1 John 4:1). The claim to have the key to the Scriptures, to possess divine utterances, to have spiritual powers are not to be *trusted* but *tested*.

What Is The Gift?

Though every believer is responsible for discerning the spirits, some have a particular power to do so. This is the gift of discernment—a special ability to distinguish between the spirit of truth and the spirit of error. A person with the gift of discernment can discriminate between that which is raised up by God and that which pretends to be. He has the ability to unmask Satan's trickery, to detect false teachings, and to ferret out false teachers. He has the ability to spot a phony before others see through his phoniness.

A person with this gift can read a religious book and almost immediately detect any subtle error. He can hear a sermon and put his finger on any deficiency of truth. He can listen to some new cultic teaching with its mixture of truth and error and not be taken in but soon sense the area of aberration. He can tell whether the atmosphere in a service is mere emotion, or emotion based on biblical truth.

When Peter affirmed the deity of Jesus, the latter recognized the divine source of his declaration. "Flesh and blood hath not revealed it unto thee, but My Father which is in heaven" (Matt. 16:17). A moment later when Peter rebuked Jesus for talking about His coming death, Jesus readily discerned the satanic source of Peter's words. "Get thee behind Me, Satan: thou art an offence unto Me: for thou savourest not the things that be of God, but those that be of men" (v. 23).

Peter's gift of discernment enabled him to see right through the deception of Ananias and Sapphira, who pretended to bring the entire proceeds from the sale of their land but in reality were turning over only part to the apostles. Peter said, "Ananias, why hath Satan filled thine heart to lie to the Holy Ghost, and to keep back part of the price of the land?" Ananias and his wife were stricken dead(Acts 5:1-10).

Simon of Samaria was baptized on profession of faith. Later, he tried to buy the power of the Holy Ghost. Again the discerning Peter saw the evil in his heart, and said, "Thy money perish with thee, because thou hast thought that the gift of God may be purchased with money. Thou hast neither part nor lot in this matter:

for thy heart is not right in the sight of God. Repent therefore of this thy wickedness . . . For I perceive that thou art in the gall of bitterness, and in the bond of iniquity" (Acts 8:20-23).

On his first missionary journey, on the isle of Cyprus, Paul's presentation of the Gospel to the deputy was interrupted by a sorcerer named Elymas who opposed Paul and tried to turn away the deputy from the faith. But Paul, filled with the Holy Spirit and doubtless exercising the gift of discernment, reprimanded the sorcerer, "O full of all subtilty and all mischief, thou child of the devil, thou enemy of all righteousness, wilt thou not cease to pervert the right ways of the Lord?" Elymas was stricken with blindness for a season (Acts 13:10, 11).

In Philippi a girl possessed with a spirit of divination, who brought her masters much gain, began to follow Paul and his company day after day, crying out, "These men are the servants of the most high God, which shew unto us the way of salvation." Paul discerned this to be an unclean spirit and ordered it out of her in the name of Jesus. Her resultant healing removed her money-making powers, which in turn incurred the wrath of her masters and brought on the arrest and beating of Paul and Silas (Acts 16:16-22).

The church of Ephesus was commended because it had tried professing apostles and discerned them liars (Rev. 2:2). But the churches of Pergamos and Thyatira were rebuked for failure to discern and root out the doctrine of Balaam (2:14) and the teachings of false prophetess Jezebel (2:20).

Perhaps this gift had greater significance in the apostolic age when the New Testament was not yet completed than it does now. How necessary it was to have those with this divinely bestowed ability to distinguish between the divine and the demonic, between truth and error. False teachers were not to be supported. "If there come any unto you, and bring not this doctrine, receive him not into your house, neither bid him God speed" (2 John 10). Still necessary today, this gift helps protect the church against the wiles of Satan who in every age transforms himself into an angel of light in the person of false teachers.

Areas in Which Discernment Operates

A teacher could be termed false on one of two counts. Either his life might be phony, or his teaching heretical. Thus, the gift of discernment penetrated both areas: the prophet's ways and the prophet's words.

The impostor-evangelist mentioned near the start of the chapter and status-seeking Ananias and Sapphira harbored impure intentions even though adhering readily to apostolic doctrine. The gift of discernment extended to motive as well as message. Interestingly, an early Christian writing from the end of the first century (the *Didache*) gives advice on ferreting out a false prophet, though he speak the truth. If he stays three days, takes anything with him except bread, asks for money, teaches the truth but does not do what he teaches, he is a false prophet.

Just as important as the prophet's ways, perhaps more critical, were the prophet's words. One acid test to determine truth as opposed to error is the same today as in apostolic days. The Apostle John states it unequivocally: "Hereby know ye the Spirit of God: Every spirit that confesseth that Jesus Christ is come in the flesh is of God: And every spirit that confesseth not that Jesus Christ is come in the flesh is not of God" (1 John 4:2, 3). Do these teachers, or their doctrine, or the spirit behind their teaching, maintain the honor of Jesus Christ? That is the test.

Every word in the test, "Jesus Christ is come in the flesh" requires attention. *Jesus* refers to the historical person.

Christ means the anointed, prophesied one. The Apostle John practically equates *Christ* with the *Deity*. "Who is a liar but he that denieth that Jesus is the Christ? He is antichrist that denieth the Father and the Son. Whosoever denieth the Son, the same hath not the Father" (1 John 2:22, 23).

Is come. This infers His preexistence. He entered the stream of history from the outside. He came down from the Father into the world. *Come* is perfect tense, indicating a definite, past accomplished act, a decisive advent, the incarnation.

In the flesh. Jesus took on Himself human nature, including a body. He became partaker of human nature that we might be sharers of His divine nature. He became incarnate that He might die on the cross for our sins. Coming in the flesh was for dying. Since Jesus Christ is spoken of in vital, living terms, the overcoming of death by resurrection is implied.

Any relegating of Jesus Christ to an inferior spot less than the incarnate Son of God, the crucified and resurrected Saviour, means that spirit is not of God.

Rev. Victor H. Ernest, a Baptist pastor who came out of spirit-ism to Christ, relates how the above test was the clinching factor that led to his conversion. Reared in a non-Christian atmosphere, he regularly attended séances. Then he came across the Bible verse, "Believe not every spirit, but try the spirits." He read that the true spirit would confess that Jesus Christ is come in the flesh. So he decided to try the spirits at the next séance, though he wasn't sure how he would go about it. To his surprise, the control spirit at the very next meeting announced that he would answer questions. This had never happened before. Each person would be allowed three questions.

Ernest directed his first question to the control spirit. "Do you believe that Jesus was the Son of God?" Smoothly came the answer that, of course, Jesus was the Son of God, and that we should believe what the Bible teaches. Never had Ernest heard a spirit affirm this, rather usually that Jesus was some great medium or a Palestinian teacher.

Before long the trumpet was back to him. This time Ernest falteringly asked, "Do you believe that Jesus is the Saviour of the world?" Immediately, almost before the question was finished, the answer came, rebuking Ernest for his doubt, then quoting authentic-sounding verses about believing.

When the trumpet returned for the final question, Ernest asked, "Spirit, you believe that Jesus is the Son of God, that He is the Saviour of the world—do you believe that Jesus died on the cross and shed His blood for the remission of sin?"

The medium, in deep trance, was hurled off his chair to the floor to lie groaning until revived. Ernest never went to another séance. He had tested the spirit to find it counterfeit. Searching God's Word, he came to know Christ. (*I Talked With Spirits,* Victor Ernest, Tyndale, Wheaton, Ill.)

Paul warned that "in the latter times some shall depart from the faith, giving heed to seducing spirits and doctrines of devils" (1 Tim. 4:1). The faith which false spirits try to sway people from believing is found in the immediately preceding verse, 1 Timothy 3:16. Again, Christ (His person and work) provides the crux of truth: "And without controversy great is the mystery of godliness: God was manifest in the flesh [incarnation], justified in the Spirit [deity declared through the resurrection—Rom. 1:4], seen of angels [resurrection attested], preached unto the Gentiles, believed on in the world, received up into glory [ascension and glorification, the divine seal on His finished work]".

Christ's incarnate Godhead and atoning ministry on the cross constitutes the major test of every creed and system. Does the teaching in question maintain the honor of the Lord Jesus Christ as Son of God and Saviour from sin? Yes, or no? The most casual application of this biblical test to many of the modern, so-called "Gospel" plays and movies would immediately reveal the inferiority of their Jesus. For example, *Jesus Christ Superstar* features a Jesus who wavered as to His own identity and who was left in the tomb. According to an Associated Press comment on the movie version of *Godspell,* the script portrays Jesus as a teacher and friend rather than a divine person. The same release referring to the movie, *The Rebel Jesus,* says it's more the Christ of Albert Schweitzer or Bishop Pike than the Christ of Billy Graham. Such truncated views of the person of Christ give unmistakable hint that the Jesus portrayed in these films is not the Christ of Spirit-breathed Scriptures.

Everybody who spouts pious phrases and smiles sweetly isn't necessarily a genuine teacher for Christ. Paul used the strongest language imaginable in the opening verses of Galatians concerning those who would preach another gospel. After a short greeting, and without any prayer or thanksgiving such as follows in most epistles, Paul launches directly into the problem at hand. He marvels that the Galatians have so soon defected from the Gospel of grace to another gospel. Judaizers, infiltrating new congregations after Paul started them, insisted that the Gospel was deficient and needed the addition of lawkeeping. Paul thundered that this was a perversion of the Gospel, then warned, "Though we, or an angel from heaven, preach any other gospel unto you than that which we preached unto you, let him be accursed" (1:8). Then so as to leave no doubt, he repeated the warning (v. 9). Any accretion to the Gospel of grace annuls the free-grace aspect, the mixture then making it a gospel of works, which is not the Gospel. Such a gospel is not of the Holy Spirit.

On Monday morning, April 25, 1907, people going to work in London, England, were shocked to see chalked on the front of the famous City Temple the word ICHABOD. The newspapers carried pictures of the unspeakable desecration in their afternoon editions. A week or so later a house painter came forward voluntarily to admit that he had chalked the word early that Monday morning. Asked in court why he had done such a sacrilegious thing, the house painter replied, "Dr. Parker told me to do it!"

Dr. Parker, the former pastor, was long since dead. The puzzled court asked for an explanation. The painter explained that he was a Christian and regular attendant at the City Temple during the days when Dr. Joseph Parker was the preacher. He told how Dr. Parker had said that if ever the false "gospel" of the higher critics was preached in that place, ICHABOD (which means "the glory is departed") should be written over the front of the building. "I did what Dr. Parker asked me to, sir."

The painter, perhaps rash in his action, was right in his discernment. Many related how Dr. Parker's successor described cherished fundamental tenets of the evangelical faith as childish things to be put away, even deriding forgiveness by blood as slaughterhouse religion.

Not everything religious should be accepted as truly Christian and biblical. To distinguish the spurious from the genuine we need discernment. We should be especially thankful for those with the gift of discernment.

Part IV
The
Signifying
Gifts

18

The Gift of Miracles

Recently religious snake-handlers in Tennessee added another daring activity—the drinking of deadly poison. At the close of an evening service at the sect's little hilltop church, two veterans of snake-handling, an assistant pastor and a layman, drank a potent mixture of strychnine and water, as the congregation chanted praises. Outside the church, after the service, the two men doubled in convulsive agony. By dawn they were dead, though many prayed over them.

The men were buried with Bibles opened to Mark 16:16-18 laid upon their stomachs. The last verse says, "They shall take up serpents; and if they drink any deadly thing, it shall not hurt them; they shall lay hands on the sick, and they shall recover."

After reading a story like this, the question everybody asks is, "What about miracles today?"

The Gospels and Acts are filled with accounts of miracles so entwined with the narrative and so woven into the message that to reject the miracles is to tear the very fabric of the entire record. For example, if the miracle of the feeding of the 5,000 be denied, how do we explain certain consequences, such as people declaring Jesus the Messiah, or desiring to make Him king, or the discussion on the Bread of Life? If miracles are eliminated, the four Gospels disintegrate. If Christ didn't rise from the dead, there's no Christian message.

Among the gifts listed in the New Testament is that of the working of miracles (1 Cor. 12:10, 28). So, we ask again, "Do people work miracles today as they did in New Testament times? If such miracles are not often being performed today, why not? And exactly what is a miracle? Are miracles of any kind happening today?"

What Is a Miracle?

The word miracle is often used quite loosely to refer to biblical wonders like raising the dead, to astronauts landing on the moon, to someone emerging from a car unhurt after crashing into a tree at 70 miles per hour, to finding a dime on the street when one is a dime short for some needed expense. Only the first example fits the biblical definition of a miracle; the other three are, in order, a greater understanding and use of the laws of science, an instance of the law of averages, and the working of divine providence.

Here's a definition of a miracle in the restricted, scriptural sense: an event of supernatural power, palpable to the senses, accompanying the servant of the Lord to authenticate the divine commission.

Three words appear most frequently in the New Testament in connection with miracles. *Power* is translated miracle 9 times. *Wonder,* occurring 16 times, always in the plural and always with *signs,* means something portentous or astonishing. *Sign,* appearing about 70 times and meaning miracle on about 60 of these occasions, has the idea of signaling or signifying. For example, the miracles in John's Gospel were to signal the deity of Christ, causing people to believe in Him. "Many other signs truly did Jesus in the presence of His disciples . . . But these [signs] are written that ye might believe that Jesus is the Christ, the Son of God; and that believing ye might have life through His name" (20: 30, 31).

These three words most used with reference to miracles each fit a different aspect of the definition.

Power—A miracle is an event of supernatural power.

Wonder—palpable to the senses.

Sign—accompanying the servant of the Lord to authenticate the divine commission.

All three words are used together in the same verse more than once in the New Testament. For example, it was said of Jesus that He was "a Man approved of God among you by miracles [power] and wonders and signs, which God did by Him in the midst of you" (Acts 2:22).

1. An event of supernatural power.

The gift of miracles involves the Spirit-given power to perform an act contrary to or superadded to natural law. C. S. Lewis points out that nature has to be interfered with by supernatural power for any event to qualify as miraculous. Because God is not a prisoner of His own natural laws, He can choose to act apart from them. A miracle is God stepping into His universe, setting aside the ordinary laws of nature to do something extraordinary. The owner of a complicated model railroad usually operated it from a control box, but on rare occasions he stepped amidst the miniature tracks to pick up by hand an engine or boxcar to reposition it. Our Creator set laws in motion by which He operates the world, but on occasion, when it serves His purpose, He has intervened to overrule some natural law. An answer to prayer, though unusual, would not qualify as a miracle unless the processes of nature were short-circuited.

The miracles of Jesus and the apostles evidenced:
> power over disease (which relates more to the gift of healing),
> power over demons,
> power over nature (stilling storm, walking on water),
> power over matter (water into wine, loaves and fishes),
> power over death

2. Palpable to the senses—a wonder.

The Mazatecs of Mexico speak of miracles as "long-necked things" because they cause people to stretch out their necks to see something amazing. *Wonder* is thought to come from the verb *watch carefully*.

To qualify as a miracle the event must be seen, or be palpable to one of the senses. Strange as it may seem and Gospel songs to the contrary, the new birth does not fit this restricted definition, for the new birth takes place within and is not observable by others at the moment of occurrence, though its results will ultimately surface.

When Jesus healed the palsied man, people were amazed (Mark 2:12). After He walked on the water, the disciples were sore amazed (6:51). At the huge catch of fish, Peter was astonished (Luke 5:9). A miracle invariably elicited a feeling of awe, stemming from the marvelous display of divine power, making people wonder.

3. Accompanying the servant of the Lord to authenticate the divine commission—a sign.

The power of a miracle made the observer wonder, signaling something significant. It authenticated the doer of the miracle as a divinely commissioned servant of the Lord. His message was validated. He was speaking for God. He should be heard and heeded.

After Jesus fed the 5,000, the people said, "This is . . . that Prophet" (John 6:14). Signs catapulted Jesus to the forefront of public view, so that He could not be hid, and witnessed to the divine authenticity of His mission. He urged people to believe His oneness with the Father "for the very works' sake" (14:11).

Likewise when Peter raised Dorcas from the dead, "it was known throughout all Joppa; and many believed in the Lord" (Acts 9:42). After Paul's miracle of pronouncing blindness on sorcerer Elymas, "the deputy . . . believed, being astonished at the doctrine of the Lord" (Acts 13:12). Apostolic miracles authenticated the apostolic message, signaling to the wondering observer that this power was of God and that the message should be heeded.

Back in chapter 3 we classified the gifts under three major categories: speaking, serving, and signifying. We have now come to the final chapters which deal with these signifying gifts: miracles, healing, tongues and interpretations. Though these gifts certainly could be listed either under speaking (tongues and interpretations) or serving (miracles and healing), we have made a separate classification because they bear a special authenticating relationship to the apostles.

Writing to the Corinthians to combat the charges of false teachers that he was not an apostle, Paul answered, among other arguments, "Truly the signs of an apostle were wrought among you in all patience, in signs, and wonders, and mighty deeds" (2 Cor. 12:12). Writing to the Romans, Paul claims that one mark of his apostolic commission was the success of his work among the Gentiles which was authenticated by the miracles Christ wrought through him. "For I will not dare to speak of any of those things which Christ hath not wrought by me, to make the Gentiles obedient, by word and deed, through mighty signs and wonders, by the power of the Spirit of God" (15:18, 19). Whoever wrote Hebrews, speaking of the apostolic group, said, "God also bearing them witness, both with signs and wonders, and with diverse miracles, and gifts of the Holy Spirit, according to His own will" (2:4). (Note that the three words most frequently used to refer to miracles are found in all these verses, namely: power, wonder, sign.)

These verses clearly state that an authenticating relationship existed between miracles and the apostles. The gift of miracles was given the apostles as evidence of their divine commission. The message of the official Twelve (and others closely associated with them who also had the gift of miracles, such as Stephen, Philip, and Barnabas) was of heavenly origin and therefore to be obeyed.

Why Were Miracles Once So Plentiful, Now So Scarce?

Miracles abounded in New Testament days. But today we do not see people walking on the water or raising the dead. This absence is either due to the unbelief of man or to the will of God.

Could it be that we stifle this gift because of our background and training? Could it be that we don't covet it sufficiently, don't have enough faith? However, some groups do hold that the gift of miracles is for today, and they advocate its practice. Would it not be logical, then, for some among these groups to possess the gift? But do we know any?

Have you ever met anyone who had the gift of working miracles? Remember—this person should be able at his word of command or prayer to suspend the laws of nature by divine power and perform some marvelous work like multiplying bread to feed thousands. Do you know of one person in your town or county who has such power at his command? If such a person existed in our state or nation, it could not be hid. If, in Jesus' day with no newspaper, radio, or TV, His miracles were noised everywhere, would not our modern, efficient media spread everywhere the supernatural ability of anyone who possessed it? Would it not be emblazoned on the 6 P.M. news? Certainly, if the gift of working miracles were sovereignly assigned by the Holy Spirit in any measurable degree today in our nation, it would soon surface to public view.

Should we then conclude that the absence of this gift may be the will of God in our day? A study of biblical miracles shows them clustering around critical periods of history; they were associated with the Exodus, the prophets, Christ and the Early Church. In each case they were wonders to signal or authenticate the servant of God. The miracles of the plagues and the manna confirmed Moses and Aaron as divinely appointed leaders. The miracles performed by the prophets, as Elijah at Mt. Carmel, established their divine commission. The miracles in the Gospels verified the heavenly mandate of Christ. The miracles which continued into the period of the apostles certified them as messengers of Christ. But miracles were the exception in biblical history. Centuries passed without occurrence of any. John the Baptist did no miracles (John 10:41). Why should it be thought strange that the Spirit not assign this gift to any extent in our day?

Could it not be that the sign gifts were given for the difficult, early years of the infant church? Who would believe the word of these ignorant and unlearned men with their fantastic story of One who rose from the dead? The apostles and early leaders were not left unaccredited. Their performance of miracles authenticated them. But when the New Testament was completed, need for such credentials diminished.

Should the gift of miracles be assigned by the Spirit today, several writers suggest that it would likely occur on mission fields where the situation would approximate that of the Early Church. Just as the Lord used miracles in the introduction of the Gospel to the first century world, so today in new territories where obstacles need to be overcome, similar palpable evidences of the truth of the Gospel may be needed to awaken the dull senses of those hearing for the first time. In countries long illuminated by the Word, miracles are not so essential. But in regions freshly open, God may sometimes suspend a law of nature to show His power over heathen idols, to give remarkable answers to simple faith, to protect His servants, and to punish scoffers. Readers of missionary reports now and again come across such instances, reminiscent of apostolic history.

Sometimes, reports of miracles from primitive areas become exaggerated. In recent years stories of multiplied and dramatic miracles in Indonesia have been circulated in Christian circles around the world. Dr. W. Stanley Mooneyham, president of

World Vision, who coordinated the Asia-South Pacific Congress on Evangelism in 1968, wrote an evaluation of these miracles. Among other things he said, "Did some miracles occur? Undoubtedly. Indonesia was in imminent danger of going Communist. The people were animists (worshipers of spirits) for the most part. Into this setting the Spirit of God wonderfully moved. Significantly, these (miracles) usually occurred in connection with fetish burning. Around these same fetishes in earlier days the witch doctors had done their own miracles. How appropriate that God would demonstrate His power as the fetishes were being burned!

"Were people raised from the dead? There is not one medically confirmed case. The two or three cases to which they would give some credence involved the persons having been 'dead' only a few hours. If trained doctors are unable to agree on when a person is clinically dead, how should these people be expected to make that critical judgment?

"People are apt to get the impression that miracles are daily occurrences even now all over Indonesia. They are not. With few exceptions the spectacular things reported are certainly not happening in Indonesia today. The miracles which did occur happened mostly on the island of Timor and principally in the period of 1965-66. Miracles occurred almost exclusively in the more animistic areas, and even there current reports indicate that these begin to drop away when the new converts get into the Scriptures. A missionary who has just returned from many years on Timor says that presently physical miracles are almost as scarce there as they are in America" ("Revival and Miracles—What About Indonesia?" *World Vision,* September 1972).

Sign-Seeking Runs Counter to Faith

Jesus acclaims faith which does not need signs. To the nobleman who wanted his son healed, Jesus said, "Except ye see signs and wonders, ye will not believe" (John 4:48). The very act of seeking a sign contradicts that which pleases God—which is faith. He said, "This is an evil generation: they seek a sign" (Luke 11:29). Jesus never reduced Himself to the level of a magician by performing a miracle to satisfy curiosity or to entertain.

When Jesus miraculously fed the 5,000, most missed the import of the sign. Instead of pondering the nature and authority of the person who could do such a wonder, they sought to make Him king merely because they saw Him as someone who could supply their daily bread. They grasped at the outward goodies but did not bow to His spiritual claims. Later when they began to understand His demands, many walked with Him no more.

Zacharias, told he was to be the father of John (the Baptist), sought a sign of confirmation. The angel answered, in effect, "Why do you doubt my message? I am Gabriel who stands in the presence of the Eternal. The sign will be dumbness till fulfilment of my word" (see Luke 1:18-20).

When Mary was told by the same angel who spoke to Zacharias that she was to be the mother of the Messiah, she humbly answered, without asking for any sign, "Behold the handmaid of the Lord; be it unto me according to thy word" (Luke 1:38).

How sad that people become much more excited over wonders in the physical realm than workings in the spiritual. How tragic to be so jaded that it takes supernatural demonstrations to arouse us. Preoccupation should not be with outward manifestations in preference to inner dealings. But reordered lives are more important than rearranged molecules. The Lord would rather we walk by faith, not by signs.

Miracles in Broader Sense

Our definition of a miracle, which involves the setting aside of the laws of nature by supernatural power, is quite restrictive. In this limited, technical sense, miracles seem a rarity today, though we admit their possibility any time God wills.

However, the denial of miracles as customary today by no means rules out wonderful occurrences: remarkable answers to prayer, extra strength, abundant provision, and timely protection. These marvelous happenings cannot be considered miracles in the narrow view because the laws of nature are not upset. But in the broader sense we call them miracles because of unusual and timely providential interference in human affairs.

One night a driver was clicking off the miles as his car sped down the highway. Soon his glassy stare fixed mechanically on the center line. Falling asleep at the wheel, he became a robot, holding the steering wheel in his loose grip. As he raced through the warm, moonlit night, suddenly a sharp pain in the side of his chest awakened him. And just in time, for looming out of the darkness toward him were two headlights.

Sensing he was on the wrong side of the road, the driver jerked his steering wheel to the right, missed by inches a huge truck whistling by, almost lost control, but managed to pull to the side. When his heart stopped pounding, he opened the door to get out. As he stood up, something fell from his lap to the grass. Stooping, he picked up the still form of a brown bird. Then he recalled the pain which had hit him in the side of his chest, awakening him just in time to avoid the crash. The sparrow had made a flight at night, which sparrows seldom do. It had darted into the open window of the speeding car, hitting him with sufficient force to arouse him. The driver knew it had been the "miraculous" split-second timing of providence. Just then the bird fluttered its wings, regained consciousness, and flew off into the night.

The Lord's dealings in the spiritual realm are much more significant than His workings in the natural domain. Calming the sea was remarkable, but not so important as stilling the tempest that storms in the heart of an anxious soul. Feeding the 5,000 was wonderful, but how much more beneficial to feed the multitudes the Bread of Life! Giving sight to a blind man was marvelous but how much more exciting for a sin-blinded man to see! Raising the dead was amazing, but beyond description is the joy of seeing a person dead in trespasses and sins receive eternal life.

Jesus' promises to His followers, "They shall take up serpents; and if they drink any deadly thing, it shall not hurt them; they shall lay hands on the sick, and they shall recover" (Mark 16:16-18) were fulfilled in the miracles of apostolic days. But Jesus' promise that His disciples would do "greater works than these" (John 14:12) is being fulfilled today. The deaf to the Word begin to hear. The lame start to walk in paths of righteousness. The purposeless become motivated to fruitful Christian living. The selfish make sacrifices. Those who wronged others make restitution. Those of whom it was said, "It would be a wonder if they ever got saved," find Christ.

These are the greater miracles.

19

The Gift
of Healing

Healings still happen, it is claimed, at Lourdes, France, where millions pass through the grotto every year in search of health. However, according to one religious editor, healings do not happen often. It almost constitutes a second miracle for a cure to be acclaimed by the Roman Catholic church as a miracle.

Strict procedures followed by the Lourdes Medical Bureau rule out any cures which mention shock, hysteria, psychosomatic or mental conditions. The healing must be organic, immediate, and complete, without any period of convalescence, and must involve a malady not at the point of cure when the patient arrived at Lourdes.

During the years 1960-1972, the Lourdes Medical Bureau handled 995 dossiers of claimed cures. The services of 2,000 doctors were used in that 12-year period to assess diagnoses and reports of cures. Of these nearly 1,000 cases, only 15 met the strict requirements necessary. Ultimately, only 7 of these 15 were deemed worthy of classification as miracles by church authorities. Though other genuine healings may have occurred, the officially proclaimed 7 to 12 years averages to slightly better than one healing every two years. (Charles Wilkinson, Editor, Religious Department, *The Spectator*, Hamilton, Ontario, Canada, Sept. 30, 1972.)

Paul speaks of the gifts of healings (1 Cor. 12:9). The double plural may indicate there are many types of cures, not only on the level of the body, but of mind as well, since an integral relationship exists between them. To some, the double plural suggests that

169

every individual healing is a direct gift from God with each cure a separate charisma.

What Is the Gift?

The gift of healing is the ability to intervene in a supernatural way as an instrument for the curing of illness and the restoration of health.

Jesus Christ, of course, is the supreme example of One in whom this gift rested. He healed in "all the cities and villages." He healed "every sickness and every disease among the people" (Matt. 9:35). He healed all who were brought in contact with Him. No instance is recorded of any sick person coming to Him and remaining sick.

The 70 messengers Jesus sent out healed. When they rejoiced that even demons were subject to them, Jesus replied that a greater cause of joy was the inscribing of their names in heaven. Judas apparently had power over sickness and demons without his name being written above.

Peter had the gift of healing, exercising it on a lame man, on those who sought his passing shadow, palsied Aeneas, even raising Dorcas from the dead (Acts 3:6-8; 5:15, 16; 9:32-41).

Healing was probably included among the great wonders Stephen did (Acts 6:8). The curing of the lame, the palsied, and those with unclean spirits is listed among the miracles of Philip (Acts 8:6, 7).

Paul healed the cripple at Lystra, wrought special curing miracles at Ephesus so that handkerchiefs and aprons which had touched his body made disease and demons depart, and on the isle of Melita healed the governor's father of flux and fever, then other sick islanders as well (Acts 14:8-10; 19:11, 12; 18:8, 9).

What the Gift Does Not Do

1. The gift does not heal every illness.

If the gift of healing could be exercised to cure every illness of a particular person, conceivably that individual would live forever. But we know that disease will ultimately do its work on every person, apart from those still alive at the return of Christ, for the sentence of death has been passed on all men. Someone facetiously commented of a man who claimed to have healing power, "His gift heals every illness but the final one."

Not only does this gift not heal the last illness of a person, but it is inoperable on many occasions. If the gift functioned all the time, why could Paul not help his close friend Epaphroditus, who was so sick he nearly died and probably was sick quite a while? (Phil. 2:25-27) Why did he not heal Timothy's chronic stomach condition instead of prescribing the medicinal use of wine? (1 Tim. 5:23) Why did he leave Trophimus ill at Miletum? (2 Tim. 4:20) These people would not have remained indisposed for any length of time if Paul's gift of healing had been employable at all times.

In fact, Paul himself was not in good health during much of his ministry (1 Cor. 2:3; 2 Cor. 11:30; 12:5, 7-10; Gal. 4:13). Instead of sending someone with the gift to heal Paul, the Lord gave him Dr. Luke as a constant companion to care for his physical needs.

2. This gift does not depend on the sick person's faith.

The concept that lack of faith prevents healing is related to the erroneous idea that sickness is the result of sin. The rabbis used to say that dropsy was due to immorality, jaundice to hatred, poverty to pride, liver trouble to backbiting, and leprosy to an evil tongue.

Some illness may indeed be the result of personal sin. Some were sick at Corinth because they abused the Lord's Supper (1 Cor. 11:30). However, though disease and death have come to the human race in general because of Adam's sin, it is a cruel hoax to claim that individual sickness is the consequence of personal sin or that a person of sufficient faith will be healed. Our Lord exploded this false theory when, asked whether a man had been born blind because of his own or his parent's sin, He stated, "Neither . . . but that the works of God should be made manifest in him" (John 9:1-3).

Many precious saints get sick and shut-in who have not committed any sin to cause illness. Was Paul's thorn in the flesh due to personal sin? Was Dorcas' fatal malady due to lack of faith? On the other hand, many openly sinning saints enjoy robust health. To say that sickness comes from personal iniquity is devastating, creating a guilt complex and leading to despairing conclusions, "I must be a bad sinner"/"I lack faith"/"I'm a poor Christian, or I'd get well."

God's main purpose for the believer is to conform him to the image of Christ. Whether or not God heals depends on whether illness or recovery best contributes to that end. Thus, the gift of healing should not be exercised on the basis of the patient's faith but on the condition of the will of God. God's sovereign plan sometimes calls for infirmity to advance divine glory and saintly maturity. Complete deliverance from bodily illness will be ours only at the resurrection of the body. How wrong to affirm that an ailing disciple is out of the will of God, or deficient in faith, if his affliction is designed to develop his faith.

3. The gift does not account for all healing.

The gift of healing requires God's power. But not all healing is divine; some is demonic, some psychic.

The powers of darkness enabled the magicians of Egypt, Jannes and Jambres, to do many unusual feats (Ex. 7:11, 12, 22; 8:7; 2 Tim. 3:8). Jesus was falsely accused of casting out demons by diabolical power (Matt. 12:24). The world of the first-century believers was full of demon-energized healers and magic workers (Acts 8:9-11; 13:8-10). Tradition says that multitudes of pagans were miraculously cured in the temple of Serapis at Alexandria, Egypt. A night's sleep by sick pilgrims in the temple in Epidaurus, Greece, reportedly healed thousands. We hear of healings performed during séances, which, from the Christian viewpoint, could well be attributed to demonic power.

Throughout the Christian era, supposed miracles of physical healing have occurred within and without the professing church, both in Roman Catholic and Protestant circles. Because of claimed curative powers resulting from alleged appearances of Mary or a saint at some particular spot, famous shrines have arisen in many parts of the world such as Lourdes in France and Fatima in Portugal. With 75% or so of illness today psychosomatic, all healings need not be classified as either divine or demonic. Many are likely psychological, or mind over matter, as in Christian Science. Someone put it, "Many are either genuine cures of imaginary ills, or imaginary cures of real ills."

The Stanford University Department of Industrial Engineering and Materials Science jointly sponsored a four-day symposium in the fall of 1972 with the Academy of Parapsychology and Medicine of Los Altos. Common to many of the presentations by specialists inquiring into the laying on of hands in healing was the argument that some mysterious form of energy can flow from one person to another. Some people, it was alleged, are capable of transferring such energy and thus can serve as healers.

In an experiment reported at this symposium, a leaf was photographed over a film plate in a dark room with a high frequency electrical current generated around the plate. In its live normal state, the leaf appeared to be filled with a myriad of tiny white bubbles seemingly bursting with energy. An injured leaf quickly develops gaping holes in this dynamic bubble pattern. But a person with healing powers or with a "green thumb" can restore the vitality of the leaf by simply laying a hand over it for a few minutes, restoring the energy bubbles within the leaf. On the other hand, a person with a "brown thumb" so treating a wounded leaf hastens the death of the leaf. According to the experimenters, in this case the energy drains out of the leaf (*New York Times*, October 8, 1972).

So, the gift of healing does not explain all cures. Summing up, black-magic conjuration openly uses the name of Satan and demonic powers. Psychic powers about which we have much yet to learn may account for some restoration to health. Also, many times God heals through answer to prayer apart from the ministry of anyone with the gift of healing, which may well be the more usual method in our day.

4. The gift does not exist equally in all centuries.

The gift seems much more prevalent in the time of Christ and the Early Church. Also, the gift seemed restricted to a few, the leaders rather than the people. Luke wrote, "By the hands of the apostles were many signs and wonders wrought among the people" (Acts 5:12). Healing was one of the sign gifts to authenticate the divine messenger. When these specially appointed divine messengers passed off the scene, need for authenticating healings decreased.

The gift may never have completely disappeared from the church, though admittedly great frauds have been perpetrated in its name. It would take a brave soul to deny the existence of this gift today, or to rule out its possibility. Who dares limit or dictate to the sovereign Spirit? He may wish to heal by means of a human instrument to whom He has granted the gift of healing.

But having said that, would we not agree that it is a rare gift today, infrequently bestowed? How many of us have personally met a person with the gift of healing? As pointed out in the previous chapter, in Jesus' day, without rapid communication and mass media, His great works were noised everywhere so that He could not be hid. In our day anyone able to heal vast numbers instantaneously of serious maladies would soon have his (or her) picture splashed all over the newspapers and TV, with vivid accounts of his sensational feats. Such a person in your town or state could not long be hid.

One person most frequently mentioned today in connection with the gift of healing is Kathryn Kuhlman, probably the best-known woman preacher in the world, with home base in Pittsburgh, Pa. For more than a quarter of a century, Miss Kuhlman has led an influential and respected ministry. Thousands have come to her services, broken in body and spirit, to go away well. Just as many come with illnesses and are not healed. If any person could be alleged to possess the gift of healing today, she would certainly seem to qualify. However, in an interview in *Christianity Today* (July 20, 1973), while admitting that few people have the gift, she disavows any such claim for herself.

The scarcity of the gift of healing may well be due to the will of God, if we recall that gifts are apportioned according to the sovereignty of the Spirit. Perhaps God has another way to handle healing. What do the epistles have to say about the subject?

The epistles never command us to heal people. One reason for a separate classification of sign gifts (miracles, healing, tongues and interpretations) is their special authenticating relationship with the apostles. Another reason is the *lack of command* for believers to do them. Most, if not all of the gifts in the speaking and serving categories, relate to areas in which we are to obey even if we do not possess the gift. For example, even if we do not have the gift of evangelism, giving, showing mercy, we are to evangelize, give, show mercy. But these sign gifts, for the certification of the apostles, are not commanded of us. Are we ever commanded to perform miracles? Are we ever commanded to heal the sick? Are we ever commanded to speak in tongues? This omission of specific command in the area of miracles, healing, and tongues helps explain why large segments of the evangelical church have not pushed these gifts. God may give these gifts when and to whom He wishes, but no one should be blamed for lack of enthusiasm in seeking these gifts.

The topic of healing receives minimal mention in the epistles. If we were obligated to seek this gift of healing which Jesus and the apostles had, certainly the New Testament writers would have so informed us in their letters. But, other than the reference to the gift of healing in 1 Corinthians 12:9, no epistle mentions healing except James. Reference is made to sickness in general (1 Cor. 15:43), and to the illnesses of communion-abusers at Corinth in particular (1 Cor. 11:30), of Epaphroditus (Phil. 2:25-27), of Timothy (1 Tim. 5:23) and Trophimus (2 Tim. 4:20). But apart from the healing of the beast's deadly wound (Rev. 13:3, 12), the only reference to literal healing of the body is in James 5:14-16. Since this is the sole citation on healing in the New Testament letters, isn't it likely that this is the definitive method of bringing restoration of health to sick saints in this age? In the absence of anyone with the gift of healing, is not this the procedure to follow? Certainly we must be concerned over the physical well-being of others even if lacking the ability to effect immediate and complete cures.

The Ministry of Healing

We've all seen signs, "In case of emergency, call . . ." The James passage says, "In case of sickness, here's what to do." Incidentally, the *existence* of illness among God's people is clearly implied.

"Is any sick among you? let him call for the elders of the church; and let them pray over him, anointing him with oil in the name of the Lord: And the prayer of faith shall save the sick, and the Lord shall raise him up; and if he have committed sins, they shall be forgiven him. Confess your faults one to another, and pray one for another, that ye may be healed" (James 5:14-16).

1. Initiative by the sick

The illness must be sufficiently serious to require the elders to come to the patient. He must be too sick to go to church, not suffering some minor complaint like a common headache.

2. Visit by the elders

The elders respond to the call of the sick man. The responsibility is on the patient to notify the leaders. Pastor and board should not be criticized for negligence if not notified of illness.

The private setting is conducive to personal counseling as well as to the mutual confession of faults. Observance of this directive would rule out publicly advertised healing campaigns where the healer knows nothing of the spiritual life of those who come for

healing. Much sensationalism, commercialism, and disillusion-
ment would be avoided.

3. Application of oil

Evangelicals are divided as to the meaning of the oil. Many
groups anoint with oil as a sacred symbol of the Spirit. Many others
believe oil means medicine. Dr. Spiros Zodhiates, General Secre-
tary, American Mission to Greeks, well versed in the Greek language and raised in the Mideast, believes the oil is medicinal. He
points out there are two words for "anoint" in Greek. *Chriō,*
from which we get Christ, or Anointed, means to anoint sacredly.
Aleiphō means "to oil," applying or rubbing oil on the body as
ancient athletes did before games to stimulate them.

Says Zodhiates, "Oil . . . was used extensively for cooking, for
lighting, and for medicinal purposes. There can be no doubt, then,
that reference is made by James to the olive oil so common
among these people of the Middle East. Even to this day, you will
find many people in the Middle East rubbing the sick with oil.
My mother used to do it to me when I was a child, but for medicinal, not religious purposes. Thus, we come to the conclusion that
James does not in any way refer to the sacred use of oil, for he uses
the verb *aleiphō* and not *chriō*. He refers instead to a good rub-
down with olive oil" (*What the Original Greek Text Says About
Healing,* Spiros Zodhiates, AMG Press, Ridgefield, N.J.). He in-
sists that the word used by James is never used in the New Testament with a sacred meaning.

Elders applied the oil because doctors were so scarce in those
days. Home remedies were first tried before a doctor was called in
from some distance. We are told Jews carried oil everywhere as a
natural means of restoring health. Physicians advised Herod, in his
final illness, to take a bath of oil. The Good Samaritan, though
not a doctor, on finding a beaten man beside the road, treated his
wounds with wine (a disinfectant) and oil for its soothing and
medicinal effect, not for any sacred anointing. Zodhiates also relates
how when his mother was too weak to rub him with oil, church
friends would be called on to come and rub him and then lead in
prayer, a common happening in that part of the world to which
James was writing.

Says Zodhiates, of James' word for anoint, "It refers rather to the
application of physical means for the relief of physical pain. In that
day it was oil; today it may be an antibiotic, or an operation, or

any other material means for the relief of physical weakness."

In this explanation, calling for the elders who used the oil is almost the equivalent of calling for the doctor in our day. Scientific techniques of modern medicine should be used. God heals through doctors. Two extremes are to be avoided. One is just to pray and refuse medical help. The other is to use physicians and never pray. The advice of James combines both pills and prayer.

David Livingstone, asked why he became a physician, replied to the effect that he wished as far as possible to imitate Jesus, but since we have not the power of doing miracles, we can do a little in the way of healing the sick; thus he sought a medical education to be like Him.

4. Prayer

The tenses are significant. Literally the text reads, "Let them pray over him, having rubbed him with oil in the name of the Lord." First, the man is to be made comfortable through medical relief. Then after doing something to relieve his ailing body, we should pray.

5. Bodily healing from the Lord our Healer

In answer to prayer the sick will be raised up. Do we not need to follow this divinely ordained procedure more than we do? Should the Spirit choose to give the gift of healing to some of His children, they should be zealous in exercising their gift. But in the seeming absence of many with such a gift today, the instructions in this classic section should be faithfully followed to benefit from God's method and ministry of healing.

6. Forgiveness

Though all illness is not due to sin, some may be. In such cases, confession to the Lord with the helpful counsel of the elders gathered around in loving support results in forgiveness and healing. Did not our Lord often bless the whole person when He healed, informing the palsied man not only to take up his bed and walk but also that his sins were forgiven? His sickness may well have been due to some sin.

Physical health should never be elevated above spiritual health. In 1907 a leading Korean evangelist, whom the missionaries were convinced had the gift of healing, announced to their surprise that he was giving up his healing ministry. He explained, "God has called me to evangelize, but people are now beginning to come to me, not to be evangelized, but only to be healed."

Worse than body sickness is soul sickness. One can afford to live and die with an ill body, but to go out into eternity with a sin-laden soul is tragic. A body with crutches thrown away or wheelchair discarded is great. But a soul with sins gone, removed as far as east is from the west, is much greater.

20

The Gifts
of Tongues
and Interpretation

An amazing religious phenomenon of our day is speaking in tongues, which, according to some observers, has now entered its third phase. Stage 1 dates back to 1906 as the date, and California as the place of the origin of modern-day tongues-speaking. For the first half-century, it was generally restricted to a few small denominations. The acceptance of the Pentecostal experience by some churches of the main line denominations began in 1960, ushering in stage 2. Since then, the utterance of ecstatic sounds, at one time confined to lower socio-economic groups, has been heard in the drawing-rooms of some dignified churchmen. Stage 3 started around 1967, when the movement took off in Roman Catholic circles. In June 1973 the seventh International Conference on the Charismatic Renewal brought 22,000 enthusiasts to Notre Dame for a three-day convention. An estimated 300,000 Catholics have turned charismatic.

Religious bookstores which a few years ago refused to carry Pentecostal writings now find them top sellers. Speaking in tongues has become an "in" practice among many Christians, privately and in small groups. On the other hand, some evangelical churches in the United States and elsewhere have been torn apart over this issue.

Paul speaks of the gift of tongues (1 Cor. 12:28, 30). What is the gift? What is its purpose? Is it for today? Is it a sign of the baptism of the Spirit? Is it a way to Christian maturity? How important is it?

What Is It?

Tongues are referred to three times in Acts, and also in a section in 1 Corinthians (12—14). In Acts, tongues seem to refer to a foreign language. The word *Pentecostal* derives from the experience on the Day of Pentecost when the 120 spoke in dialects, not their native tongues and not learned through the normal educative process, so that people from many nations round about heard the message, each in his own language (Acts 2:1-13).

The tongues-speaking at Cornelius' home (Acts 10:44-47) also likely involved definite foreign languages since Peter called it "the like gift" as came on Pentecost (11:15-18). When the disciples of John the Baptist at Ephesus came into knowledge about Christ and spoke in tongues, it would seem to be the same miracle of speaking in foreign dialects (19:1-7).

Many, who would agree that tongues in the three episodes in Acts refers to definite languages, hold that tongues-speaking in 1 Corinthians 12—14 is of a different nature. These tongues are thought to be ecstatic utterances which do not correspond to any known language. Learned scholars differ on the issue. When this author examined 10 commentaries on 1 Corinthians, five said tongues were definite languages as at Pentecost and five said tongues were ecstatic utterances. Perhaps this debate cannot be indisputably resolved.

If tongues at Corinth were ecstatic utterances, this type of tongues-speaking should not, strictly speaking, be called Pentecostal, for at Pentecost the speaking was in definite foreign languages. At Pentecost, instead of erecting new language barriers, the existing linguistic obstacles were removed as each heard in his own tongue. Much modern tongues-speaking (the ecstatic utterance type) does just the opposite by erecting a linguistic barrier, which without interpretation cannot be overcome.

The gift of interpretation, when the tongue was a foreign language, would be the ability to translate by someone who did not know the language. In the case of ecstatic utterance, the gift would be to interpret the non-linguistic sounds.

Purpose of the Gift

The major purpose of glossolalia (speaking in tongues) in Acts seems to have been evidential: that is, to authenticate the Gospel messengers. At Pentecost tongues-speaking attracted a crowd, provided a springboard for Peter's sermon, and helped win 3,000 souls.

After the Gospel was preached to Jews at Pentecost, the next major step in its spread was preaching it to Gentiles at Cornelius' house. This major innovation needed divine authentication. Tongues were used to convince the skeptical Jewish believers that the Gospel was for Gentiles too.

Again at Ephesus when Christ's finished work was declared to the dozen followers of John the Baptist, who had heard only of the forerunner, tongues offered evidence of the reality of Paul's new message. Tongues, "a sign, not to them that believe, but to them that believe not" (1 Cor. 14:22), gave divine endorsement to this new line of apostolic action. Thus, tongues deserve a place among the sign gifts.

However, if at Corinth tongues were ecstatic speech, their value was directed inward, toward the speaker, for others did not know what was said. To qualify as a gift, a Spirit-given ability must be directed outward, to others, edifying the church. Thus, uninterpreted tongues-speaking, though some sort of a spiritual exercise, falls short of being a gift, for it edifies only the speaker. But tongues-speaking, when interpreted, is elevated to the equivalent of prophecy, for then it edifies. "He that speaketh in an unknown tongue edifieth himself; but he that prophesieth edifieth the church" (1 Cor. 14:4). To restate, ecstatic speaking fails to reach the status of a gift, unless interpreted and thus edifying.

Limitations on Tongues

Some evangelicals hold that the gift of tongues (along with miracles and healings) should be considered sign gifts which mainly served to authenticate the early apostolic leaders and then ended once for all. To class all tongues-speaking today as spurious is daring, dangerous, and a denial of the right of the sovereign Spirit to endow His servants with whatever gift He pleases. However, we point out the following limitations.

1. Tongues are not the sign of baptism in the Spirit.

Some hold that unless a person speaks in tongues he has not received the baptism of the Spirit. This can stir up pride and division in a church by creating a super-status class looking down on an inferior group. Many of God's choicest saints who never spoke in tongues, some of whom we shall name later, would be relegated to second-class rating.

Isn't it significant that in the major section dealing with gifts (1 Cor 12—14) Paul points out that all believers have been baptized in the Spirit (12:13), not just those who have one particular gift of the Spirit? Since all Christians have been baptized, but not all speak in tongues, tongues could not be the sign of baptism in the Spirit.

Apart from the verse in the previous paragraph, the only other references to the baptism in the Holy Spirit, six in number, are virtually one in that they are a quotation of the words of John the Baptist spoken prophetically, "I indeed baptize you with water unto repentance; but He that cometh after me is mightier than I, whose shoes I am not worthy to bear, He shall baptize you with the Holy Ghost" (Matt. 3:11, see also Mark 1:8; Luke 3:16; John 1:33; Acts 1:4, 5; Acts 11:15, 16). Fulfillment of John's prediction came on the Day of Pentecost, a once-for-all historical event like the birth of Christ, when the exalted Jesus Christ at the Father's right hand gave the Holy Spirit in the name of the Father and in fulfillment of the promise (Acts 1:4; 2:33). The baptism in the Spirit is never mentioned outside these references.

Some allege that the baptism of the Spirit will be given to believers who ask for it, as did the disciples in the upper room between the Ascension and Pentecost. But there is no record of the 120 asking for the Spirit in those 10 days of waiting. Pentecost did not come through marvelous prayers, or through the fulfillment of conditions, or through meeting some cost by the disciples. There was no laying down of any series of steps which had to be first observed. Nor was there any subjunctive, "you might be baptized," but a simple, direct, future indicative. The Spirit came suddenly on the entire group, who were not on their knees but sitting (Acts 2:2).

Nowhere are believers commanded to seek the baptism of the Spirit. At regeneration every believer is baptized in the Spirit into the body of Christ. If a person has not been baptized in the Spirit, he is not in the body of Christ, and unsaved, for there's no other way of entering Christ's body. If he is in the body he has been baptized in the Spirit. Here is the reason for absence of any command in the Bible urging believers to seek the baptism of the Spirit. Why search for what they already have received at the outset of their Christian life? For the Christian to ask for the Spirit's baptism is like a married man asking his wife to marry him. Though the baptism of the Spirit is a once-for-all occasion, the filling of the Spirit may be a repeated action. That's why believers are commanded to be filled with the Spirit (see Eph. 5:18).

Note again that at the outset of the discussion on gifts, Paul declares that all believers have been "baptized into one body" (1 Cor. 12:13). Then he points out that not all speak in tongues. Thus, tongues cannot be the sign of baptism.

2. *Tongues are not the biblical method of Christian growth.*

People hunger for reality. Some have been robbed of their faith by biblical critics. Some are emotionally starved in churches not famed for their spirituality. Some are dissatisfied at their personal barrenness. Some are tired of fighting in their churches. Others have a natural curiosity, fanned by people who suggest that more is available in the Christian life. All these people are open to the tongues movement, especially when its proponents claim the practice gives renewed devotion, deeper prayer life, intimate communion with God instead of theoretical knowledge, decrease of tension and increase of peace and joy.

Two things need to be said. First, all these benefits may be and are experienced by many believers by the working of the Spirit in their lives apart from tongues-speaking.

Second, the Bible does not indicate that tongues-speaking is the way to grow in the Christian life. On the contrary, tongues-speaking is never once mentioned after Acts except in 1 Corinthians 12—14. In all explanations of life in the Spirit in all New Testament epistles, tongues-speaking is completely ignored. If tongues provided the key to Christian growth, would they never be advocated?

Sanctification is not a sudden acquisition of spiritual maturity by an exciting emotional experience. It is a growth process by which moral likeness to Jesus Christ is produced by the indwelling power of the Holy Spirit. No psychological substitute achieves spiritual maturity.

3. *Tongues are not the exclusive domain of Christianity.*

Charismatics readily admit that some tongues-speaking is of the devil, also that some may be spurious and counterfeit. Tongues-speaking has been reported from the days of Plato, known among the Zulus, practiced in Hinduism. A convert from Hinduism, told that his Christianity was not real because he had not spoken in tongues, replied, "I have only to go down to the local Hindu temple to hear tongues-speaking." Tongues-speaking has been heard among Muslims, Mormons, and spiritualist mediums, not to mention various other groups.

Since it can be done by non-Christians, tongues-speaking cannot be the sure sign of one's faith in Christ, much less of the baptism in the Spirit.

4. Tongues are not the sign of maturity or spirituality.

It's possible to have this gift while living a carnal life. The Corinthian church which shone in this gift also was marked by immaturity, causing Paul more headaches and heartaches than any other church.

In the middle of his discussion on gifts (1 Cor. 12—14), Paul detours to pen the famous chapter on love (13). Without love, gifts profit nothing, including tongues. "Though I speak with the tongues of men and of angels, and have not charity, I am become as sounding brass, or a tinkling cymbal" (v. 1). What all believers should emphasize is not the gifts but the graces of the Spirit. The mark of spirituality is not tongues-speaking but fruit-bearing. Not the babble of unknown tongues, but the beauty of a consistent life, is what counts. Boasting of one's gifts—whether tongues or any other—violates the principle of love. Christlike character looms much more important than tongues-speaking. As one man put it, "I don't care how high a man jumps or how loud he hollers, if when he lands on the ground he walks straight."

If tongues are a sign of mature spirituality and God's best for one's life, isn't it strange that the following spiritual giants never spoke in tongues: Augustine, Calvin, Luther, Knox, Wesley, Whitefield, Bunyan, Jonathan Edwards, Finney, Wycliffe, Carey, George Müller, Hudson Taylor, Adoniram Judson, Spurgeon, Moody, Billy Sunday, Billy Graham, to name a few?

5. Tongues are not a church-building gift.

Not only must gifts be exercised in love, but they must also build up the saints. Because ecstatic speech in the church service is incomprehensible and thus unhelpful (unless interpreted), Paul rates the gift of prophecy far superior to tongues. "He that speaketh in an unknown tongue speaketh not unto men, but unto God: for no man understandeth him. . . . But he that prophesieth speaketh unto men to edification, and exhortation, and comfort" (1 Cor. 14:2, 3). Gifts are not given for psychological value, subjective spiritual exercise, nor self-aggrandizement, but for the strengthening of other believers. This is why Paul in the church would rather speak five words with his understanding than 10,000 in a tongue. The overriding consideration in the exercise of each gift is, *does it equip the church?* In fact, as pointed out earlier, tongues-speaking apart from interpretation does not qualify as a gift because of its failure to profit others.

No instruction is given concerning the private use of tongues, but specific strictures are listed for public practice. Unbelievers coming into a group speaking in tongues will conclude these people "are mad," whereas if outsiders come into a group where clear preaching of Christ is the practice, they may be convicted by the understandable Word of God (1 Cor. 12:24). If the church does practice tongues in the service, then an interpreter must be present; otherwise the tongues-speaker must keep silent (1 Cor. 14:28). Well do I remember sitting on the platform of a large California church many years ago when suddenly in the midst of the pastor's sermon a lady jumped to her feet and spoke ecstatically. The pastor paused till she finished, then asked, "Is there an interpreter?" When no one spoke, he continued the sermon. Either she was out of order scripturally, or some interpreter failed to do his job.

Another regulation for public use concerns orderliness. Only two or at the most three are to speak in one service, and then they are to speak in turn. Each tongues-speaking has to be immediately followed by interpretation, in alternate fashion. Paul is virtually saying that tongues-speaking does not fit the pattern of a God who wants to make Himself known to others in a Christian gathering, almost restricting it to one's personal life.

Elmer L. Towns, in his book *America's Fastest Growing Churches*, (Impact Books, Nashville, Tenn., 1972) points out that eight of ten strongly oppose speaking in tongues. The charismatic movement is not the only growing branch of Protestantism.

6. Tongues are not the test of ecumenicity.

Amazingly, tongues-speaking seems to have become a rallying-point for ecumenicity. People from dozens of denominations gather together, not on the basis of the major doctrines of the Christian faith but on an experience: tongues-speaking. How strange that something that has been done by Mormons, Muslims, unconverted Zulus, and spiritualists becomes a test of fellowship among Christians!

Furthermore, how can tongues-speaking be a basis for ecumenicity with people of unitarian persuasion? According to Vincent Synan in his book *The Holiness Pentecostal Movement* (Eerdmans, Grand Rapids, Mich.), Pentecostal unitarians, known as *Jesus Only People* because they believe Jesus to be the only Person in the Godhead, numbered half a million in the United States less than 10 years ago. These people speak in tongues. Yet they deny the distinct personality of the Father and of the Holy Spirit. Can such a movement be received into full Christian fellowship just because they speak in tongues? It would seem that ecumenicity ought to be based on something more substantial, especially when radically divergent beliefs are involved.

Fellowship with Roman Catholics on the basis of tongues is also problematic. One major doctrine involved in the Reformation was justification by faith. Rome teaches that a person must supply merits of his own to add to the merits of Christ, in order to be acceptable to God. This has been known as the doctrine of infused righteousness. Reformation theology taught imputed righteousness, that the believer is justified at the time of his believing, declared so by reason of Christ's merits, for he has no righteousness of his own.

Dr. Harold Lindsell puts it this way, "The question of justification by imputed righteousness through faith cannot be sidestepped. Any speaking in tongues that is worthy of the name must be based upon a credible salvation, and there can be no salvation that is not based upon justification by faith alone. Without justification by faith alone there can be no valid tongues-speaking, Catholic, Protestant, or any other brand. For Pentecostals to accept Catholic charismatics as bona fide believers because they have spoken in tongues is to put the cart before the horse. Tongues do not prove the speaker has been justified. Acceptance in the Christian community must be based not upon tongues but upon the acceptance of imputed righteousness of Christ through faith alone" ("Tests for the Tongues Movement," copyright 1972 by *Christianity Today*).

Besides justification by faith alone, other doctrines held by Catholics which Protestants do not find in the Bible include the sacrifice of the Mass, the infallibility of the Pope, penance, and indulgences. Strangely, some Catholics claim to have been *strengthened* in these unbiblical beliefs through tongues-speaking. One priest wrote, "The traditional devotions of the Church have taken on more meaning. Some people have been brought back to a frequent use of the sacrament of penance through the experience of the baptism in the Spirit. Others have discovered a place for devotion to Mary in their lives, whereas previously they had been indifferent or even antipathetic toward her. One of the most striking effects of the Holy Spirit's action has been to stir up devotion to the Real Presence in the Eucharist" (*Pentecost in the Catholic Church*, Edward O'Connor, Dove Publications, Pecos, N.M.).

At the International Conference on the Charismatic Renewal at Notre Dame in June 1973, Cardinal Suenens, declared that "unity with the Spirit is unity with Mary, the holy mother" (*Newsweek*, June 25, 1973).

How could the Holy Spirit who inspired the Bible be the same Spirit who would lead people to support doctrines that run counter to His own teachings in the Bible? Ecumenicity must not be based on tongues-speaking but on the inscripturated, Spirit-breathed Word of God.

Some Observations

1. Avoid being discontented with God's normal workings in us.

No Christian should feel threatened because he has not spoken in tongues, providing he is growing in grace and exhibiting the fruit of the Spirit in character and witness.

Most New Testament Christians had no recorded experience of tongues, including the 3,000 converted at Pentecost, the lame man, Stephen, Barnabas, Silas, Dorcas, Sergius Paulus, the Philippian jailer, Crispus, Apollos, Aquila, Priscilla. Though the argument from silence is always inconclusive, the impression of the Early Church is not that of a group of Christians known for their ability to speak in tongues, but rather of a bold band who turned the world upside down through their clear preaching in understandable language.

2. Accept tongues-speaking as a New Testament gift.

At the annual meeting of the Christian Reformed Church in the summer of 1973 at Grand Rapids, Mich., it was reported that a dozen Christian Reformed ministers quietly claim to have had charismatic experiences. The synod, rejecting the "second blessing" baptism of the Holy Spirit as unbiblical, ruled that both clergy and laity who claim such experiences are to be accepted as long as they do not press their claims in such a way that would neither contradict other teachings of Scripture nor disrupt the peace of the church.

Paul did not claim that all tongues-speaking was spurious or due to overemotionalism. He ended his discussion urging brethren to covet prophecy, but not prohibit tongues. "Forbid not to speak with tongues" (1 Cor. 14:39). He himself spoke in tongues.

Even though we may believe the gift served its major purpose in apostolic days, we dare not try to put a strait jacket on the Holy Spirit to confine Him within the borders of our traditional mold. The Spirit can give His gifts when and where He wills.

Does every congregation need every gift? C. Peter Wagner answers, "It must be remembered that the body of Christ is universal, with many local manifestations. Spiritual gifts are given to the body universal, and therefore certain ones may or may not be found in any particular local part of the body. This explains why, for example, a local church or even an entire denomination may not have been given the gift of tongues, while other parts of the body might have it" (*Frontiers in Missionary Strategy,* Moody Press, Chicago, Ill.).

3. Beware of majoring in the minors.

If this chapter does not ardently advocate tongues-speaking, it's because this approach seems harmonious with Paul's treatment of the subject. In his major section dealing with this theme (1 Cor. 12—14), Paul never directed the Corinthians to seek this particular gift. Rather, he diplomatically substituted other goals. In chapter 12 he stressed the need for all the gifts; in chapter 13 the indispensability of love; in chapter 14 the superiority of prophecy.

Nor did Paul ever suggest to any other church to seek tongues. Isn't it revealing that Paul never mentions tongues in any epistle outside Corinthians, where he soft-pedals it and tries to correct its abuses? In writing of the Spirit-controlled life in all his other epistles, Paul completely ignores tongues. We would never have learned that Paul himself spoke in tongues, had he not told us so in rebuking the excesses of this practice. If tongues-speaking were of prime importance, certainly the Spirit would have led Paul to write about it somewhere else. After Acts, only one book mentions tongues—*and as a problem.* Contrasting the large amount of teaching on the Holy Spirit with the minute amount on tongues, one is led to conclude that tongues are relatively unimportant.

For this gift to be singled out for emphasis, and to be the rallying-point of international conventions, seems majoring in the minors.

4. Recognize God's overruling sovereignty.

Dr. Russell Hitt, editor of *Eternity,* in an article on the "New Pentecostalism," reports that many of his friends now glow with a new radiance through wonderful experiences with the Holy Spirit. Though he accepts their testimony as valid and deeply moving, he finds the going rough in trying to square the phenomenon with the teaching of the Scriptures. Hitt comments, "How do you formulate correct Christian doctrine? Do you interpret the Bible by your experience, or your experience by the Bible? You must start with the Bible, not experience. We must judge all teaching by the Word of God. Many who have had a recent 'Pentecostal' experience have trouble giving a proper Scriptural explanation for what has happened. Instead they testify to an experience, and build up a strange framework of teaching from the book of Acts for the questionable doctrine of 'the baptism of the Spirit.' " Hitt's conclusion: the tongues experience may be a psychological manifestation through which God has somehow deigned to work.

Also, God may overrule in another way. Initial interest in the person of the Holy Spirit on the level of experience or curiosity by those looking for the unusual may lead to a study of the Spirit's writings. More than once God has used surprising methods to bring reformation. Meditation on the truth of God's Word has led many to forsake teachings that cannot be substantiated from the Bible.

Out of the renewed and widespread interest in the Holy Spirit, God may override with another benefit. Since the purpose of the Holy Spirit is to exalt the Lord Jesus Christ, proper study of this topic will lead to the honor and glory of our blessed Lord.

5. Emphasize the need for proclaiming the Word in understandable speech.

Communication seems to be a key word in our day. Paul pointedly stated the superiority of prophecy, the clear presentation of a divine message in the language of the hearer, over incomprehensible, ecstatic speech. The highest honor, the greatest news, the chief joys, all belong to those who proclaim the unfathomable riches of Christ. Tongues erect a barrier between speaker and hearer, but the person empowered by the Spirit to speak in the vernacular of the listener can help break the power of cancelled sin and set the prisoner free.

The Christian and Missionary Alliance has twice faced the tongues question in official capacity, in 1907 and again in 1963. Its position, twice affirmed, succinctly summarizes a wise attitude, "Seek not, forbid not."

Part V
Putting Your Gifts to Work

21

How to
Discover Your Gifts

On a trip around the world a man and his wife arrived in Switzerland for a three-day stay. Checking tired into their hotel in late afternoon, they decided to eat in the hotel dining room. The evening dinner was excellent but expensive. When they asked the waiter to add the cost to their hotel bill, he nodded consent, smiling in a knowing way.

To save money the couple ate most meals out, but never had as fine food as that first evening. Receiving their hotel bill at the end of their stay, they noticed they had not been charged for that fine dinner. They learned, to their chagrin, that payment of advance reservations had included not only room but meals as well. They could have eaten every meal for all three days in the hotel dining room at no extra cost.

How like many Christians! Unaware of what wealth the Holy Spirit has given them in the form of "spiritual gifts," they go through life without using their resources. In the day of judgment will we not be asked, among other questions, "How faithfully have you exercised your gifts?" If so, doesn't it behoove every believer to endeavor earnestly both to discover and develop those gifts?

The Apostle Paul urges us to uncover and utilize our gifts. He exhorts every believer "not to think of himself more highly than he ought to think; but to think soberly" (Rom. 12:3). Though *think* occurs three times in the English translation, the word *soberly* is also a form of the verb *think*, which was used in the ancient world to describe a man in his right mind. Thus, with four trip-hammer blows we are told to think sanely. This sound thinking is to correspond to the measure of faith dealt us by God, which is usually equated to mean the gifts given each individual by God. A sensible estimate of our abilities is a spiritual necessity. Neither haughtiness nor self-denigration should hinder a believer from proper appraisal of his gifts.

But how do we go about discovering our spiritual capacities? Here are seven suggestions. Perhaps nominating committees, seeking guidance in selection of church officers, can profit from these principles.

Delineation: List the Gifts

A jeweller who would recognize various gems must become acquainted with all kinds of gems. Similarly, the Christian must be informed about the many, multiformed New Testament gifts if he would hope to recognize his own. Nineteen gifts have been cataloged and discussed in previous chapters.

You likely have more than one gift. Timothy had several including prophecy, teaching, evangelism, exhortation, and perhaps others. Gifts in any church may be more plentiful than we think. For example, the mention of the prayer of faith on the part of elders for the recovery of the seriously ill (James 5:15) presupposes the presence of the gift of faith in the leadership of every church. Also in every church the gift of teaching would have to be possessed by many, as would the gift of evangelism, and many others. That's why this chapter title reads, "How to Discover Your Gifts."

Perhaps we have overrated the nature of gifts by thinking of them as something impressive when in reality they may be quite ordinary. Instead of flamboyant, grandstand abilities, they may be silent, steady workings of the Holy Spirit who does not come in earthquake, storm, or wind, but in the still, small voice and soft, simple way.

Any individual gift may be channeled into a multitude of ministries by different people. The gift of teaching may be used by one person to teach children, by another for youth, by another for college students, by still another for seminarians. Discovery of our own combination of personal gifts and particular ministries may lead us into a specific, even special, almost unique pattern of service.

How tragic for gifts to lie dormant for years, like some masterpiece hidden in an attic! Failure to recognize a gift doesn't annul its existence. Nor does ignorance of a gift lessen its value.

We are responsible to discover our gifts. More than once Timothy was exhorted to keep that good thing committed him by the Holy Spirit (1 Tim. 6:20; 2 Tim. 1:14), which would doubtless include his gifts. Archippus was told to take heed to the ministry received from the Lord and to fulfill it (Col. 4:17).

May not failure to find and foster our gifts be one way of quenching the Spirit?

Doing of Service: Go to Work

Even if we thought we had no gifts, or were unaware of our responsibility to discover and develop our gifts, we do possess hundreds of New Testament commands which operate in the area of gifts. Everyone, without possessing the following gifts, is enjoined to evangelize, exhort, show mercy, and help. As we begin to obey in these or other spheres, the Holy Spirit gradually unveils certain gifts. So we should get busy in Christian service.

When D. L. Moody moved to Chicago as a young believer, he sought some Christian activity to fill up his spare time. He was directed to North Wells Sunday School in a poor part of the city. The next Sunday morning Moody walked to the corner of Wells Street and Chicago Avenue to ask the superintendent for some work. He didn't even ask for a class, for he said in those days he couldn't teach. The superintendent casually told Moody to go out into the streets and alleys and round up whatever boys he could find. Both the superintendent and Moody were unaware where this Christian activity would lead. But by exposing himself to helping where he could, Moody progressed to teaching, then to evangelism, and ultimately to founding the famed Moody Bible Institute virtually on the very site of his early service.

Updating to a contemporary evangelist—on a Lake Michigan boat ride sponsored by Chicagoland Youth for Christ back in the '40s, a few young people, wandering from deck to deck and from stem to stern, came across a young man with blonde hair and penetrating blue eyes who was energetically preaching to a handful of youth. The speaker was Billy Graham. He was not yet famous. His audience was small. But as he had been doing since his conversion in the teens, he was going at it with gusto and zeal.

At conversion the Holy Spirit grants gifts to every child of God and assigns a ministry. But first must come spiritual preparation. The extent to which the divine design is fulfilled depends on the believer's faithfulness. Hence, he should go to work immediately. Though Paul was commissioned to his ministry to the Gentiles on the Damascus Road and given gifts commensurate, a few years elapsed before he began this ministry in full force. Doubtless Paul was busy in service in the Tarsus area when Barnabas went searching for help for the new Gentile ministry at Antioch. That year of service at Antioch also helped prepare Paul for his missionary journeys to Gentiles and kings.

We ought to expose ourselves to various kinds of Christian service, perhaps first in the area of natural abilities. Perhaps we should try teaching a Sunday School class, attend teacher training, visit door-to-door, join a nursing-home team, take in a Lay Institute for Evangelism. Some proficiency in an area may suggest a potential gift. Dr. Charles C. Ryrie says, "Many ordinary laymen and women miss the full use of their gifts simply because they will not tie themselves down to a regular Sunday School class or even to a simple administration job in the church. We must be unreservedly willing to do anything if we would know the fullest use of our spiritual gifts" (*Balancing the Christian Life,* Moody Press, Chicago, Ill.).

Joan, an inarticulate introvert, forced herself to join a visitation team. The first evening she was naturally hesitant to speak. But on her second night she found herself uttering appropriate words on each visit. Thoughts which brought real help to the hearer seemed to pop into her head at the right moment. Continuation of this pattern brought her the conviction that she possessed the gift of encouragement.

On the other hand, Bob was elected to an office in the men's fellowship, which provided opportunity for the exercise of the gifts of leadership. But no gift was evident during his term of office. He insisted on a different task when his term expired. Not that one should quit the first time he falls flat on his face. A few failures may be required before a gift is developed.

Willingness to try something new may uncover a gift we never knew we possessed. Or urging by fellow believers to some different Christian service may suggest a hitherto hidden spiritual ability. When Paul encouraged Timothy to do the work of an evangelist, was he hinting that such activity might bring out the gift of evangelism and thus help fill to fuller measure Timothy's ministry? (2 Tim. 4:5) When considering whether to engage in some form of Christian work, adopt the well-known slogan, "Try it—you may like it!"

Desire: Note Your Inclinations

How does a person discover his singing talent? He finds he is drawn toward singing, and toward those who have vocal ability. If a person has piano-playing talent, he probably is drawn toward the keyboard and bangs out a few songs. So with spiritual gifts. A person is drawn toward a certain area of service. Desire for a gift may well point up the existence of that gift.

In addition, desire for a specific gift suggests that an outlet will be provided for the ministry of that gift. To a degree, gifts shape our future. With a God of order, desire, gift, and calling are related.

Looking at the relationship in reverse, when God wants some ministry performed, He will certainly equip His chosen child with a corresponding gift. And along with the gift, He will incline that person's heart in the direction of that gift. Strong desire for a gift may well signal its possession. Or, to state it another way, a gift will usually be preceded by desire and followed by opportunity to use it.

Adoniram Judson, pioneer missionary to Burma, took on a comparatively new convert in a minor, paid position of assistant, even though two other converts showed superior speaking ability and mental keenness. He told why he favored Moung Shwa-ba over the others. "The principal trait of character which distinguishes him from the rest, and affords considerable evidence that he is called by higher authority than that of man to the Christian ministry, is his humble and persevering desire for that office—a desire which sprang up in his heart soon after his conversion and which has been growing ever since. I intend to employ him, at present, as an assistant on a small allowance of eight rupees a month. In that situation he will have an opportunity of improving in those qualifications which are requisite to fit him to be a teacher of religion among his fellow-countrymen."

Judson's confidence was not misplaced. He later wrote in his diary, "I find Moung Shwa-ba a most valuable assistant in all parts of missionary work." (*The Life of Adoniram Judson,* Edward Judson, ABPS, 1883) What led Judson to choose him over others? His humble and persevering desire to exercise that particular gift.

We are commanded to desire the best gifts. "Covet earnestly the best gifts" (1 Cor. 12:31). "Desire spiritual gifts, but rather that ye may prophesy" (1 Cor. 14:1). "This is a true saying, If a man desire the office of a bishop, he desireth a good work" (1 Tim. 3:1).

The commands to desire the best gifts raise a problem. How do we reconcile these commands with the clear teaching that the Holy Spirit sovereignly assigns the gifts to whomever He chooses? Here are two observations. First, the commands to desire the greater gifts are collective commands, pertaining to the whole church more than to individual believers. To function smoothly, a body, though requiring all parts, has special need of important members. The Corinthian church, unlike a healthy body, had been majoring in the lesser gifts and minoring in the better ones. Hence the command to desire the better. Without the great gifts, the church would seriously suffer.

A second observation—the desire in an individual for a gift does not guarantee it. The overriding factor is the will of the Holy Spirit. Final assignment belongs to Him who allots to every individual believer as He chooses (1 Cor. 12:11; Heb. 2:4). Strong desire for a gift we never discover in ourselves should lead us to conclude that other motives have somehow clouded our hearts. We must place ourselves under the hand of the Spirit, assured that He will entrust to us that gift He desires us to use. Then His desire will blend with our desire.

Dedication

You are trying to discover your gifts, so you have reviewed the list of various gifts mentioned in the New Testament.

By obeying biblical commands you have been doing service in the areas of several gifts.

You have found yourself drawn toward one or more of these gifts. This desire may well indicate possession of a gift or gifts.

Perhaps at this point it would be well to dedicate yourself and these potential gifts to the Lord.

Ever notice the location of Paul's discussion of gifts in Romans? It comes at the very beginning of the practical section that deals with godly living—right after he asks for dedication of the believer's body.

Most of Paul's epistles break into two main divisions: first doctrinal, then practical. His usual procedure is to lay a basis of belief on which to urge beauty of behavior. It's doctrine, then duty. Romans, following this pattern, contains first a solid foundation of teaching on the theme of salvation, then appeals to dedication and devotion of life commensurate with this wonderful redemption. Here's the appeal at the start of the practical section, "I beseech you therefore [on the basis of the truth of salvation presented in previous chapters], brethren, by the mercies of God [mercies of justification, sanctification, and inevitable glorification outlined in earlier chapters], that ye present your bodies a living sacrifice, holy, acceptable unto God, which is your reasonable service. And be not conformed to this world; but be ye transformed by the renewing of your mind, that ye may prove what is that good, and acceptable, and perfect will of God" (Rom. 12:1, 2).

Then, immediately after this appeal for dedication, Paul turns to the subject of gifts (vv. 3-8). Is he trying to tell us that after an act of general dedication the first specific area that needs dedication is our gifts?

How appropriate, then, as one begins to discover a gift or gifts, to dedicate them to the Saviour. How fitting to consciously place such gifts in the Lord's service, expressing willingness to obey Him with our spiritual capacities.

We need this step of commitment.

Development
We are to be instruments, not ornaments. Consecrating a gift should lead to its cultivation. Desire for a gift should lead to its dedication, then to its development.

A literal translation of the passage on the seven gifts in Romans 12:6-8 contains no main verb: "Whether prophecy, according to the measure of faith; or service, in serving; or the one teaching, in teaching; or the one exhorting, in exhorting; or the one giving in singleness of mind; the one governing, in diligence; the one showing mercy, in cheerfulness." But the choppy style of the Greek demands amplification to describe the use of the gifts in English. The Authorized version supplies verbs (indicated by italics) for three of the gifts, whereas some modern paraphrases supply verbs for all seven gifts. The following expansion points up our responsibility for developing our gifts. "If our gift is preaching, let us preach to the limit of our vision. If it is serving others, let us concentrate on our service; if it is teaching, let us give all we have to our teaching; and if our gift be the stimulating of the faith of others, let us set ourselves to it. Let the man who is called to give, give freely; let the man who wields authority think of his responsibility; and let the man who feels sympathy for his fellows act cheerfully" (Phillips).

The existence of a gift is a call to exercise it. Eyes are purposeless unless they exercise the function of sight. Paul advised Timothy, "Neglect not the gift that is in thee" (1 Tim. 4:14). Weymouth translates this, "Do not be careless about the gifts with which you are endowed." And he continues in the next verse, "Habitually practice these duties and be absorbed in them so that your growing proficiency in them may be evident to all" (v. 15). Paul also told Timothy to make full proof of his ministry (2 Tim. 4:5). Faithful utilization of a gift brings increased effectiveness in its ministry, but failure to develop a gift curtails one's service.

Disuse of a limb results in paralysis or atrophy, so doctors order patients up soon after surgery. Similarly, exercise is the only way to prevent a gift's lapse or collapse. If you don't use it, you lose it.

Gifts have been likened to seeds which start small and bloom with proper care. Nurtured by love, they develop into effective instruments. Cultivation of a gift may mean formal training in some suitable school. A student with the gift of teaching who subjects himself to the discipline of Greek language study, other things remaining equal, will become a more proficient teacher.

Development of a gift may involve one in formal study, at home by correspondence, in Sunday School, or in evening Bible school.

Our gifts may be sharpened through the ministry of the gifts of fellow Christians. One reason Paul wished to travel to Rome was to bestow the benefit of his spiritual gifts, the overflow of which would contribute to the edification of believers (Rom. 1:11). But for Paul's gifts to benefit any Roman believer, that person had to pay attention, hearing and heeding. If his mind wandered, Paul's gifts would yield minimal value.

The mutuality of gifts and ministry Paul indicated in the next verse. He would also receive strength from Roman Christians (v. 12). Thus, the ministry of edification is a never ending process.

Gifted believers minister to others, who, thereby edified, exercise their abilities in the service of others, who in turn strengthen others, and so on. None of us gets to the point where he cannot benefit from the spiritual ministries of others.

Significantly, the development of one gift may lead to the discovery of another. Philip, chosen for the equitable distribution of alms because of his wisdom, went on to exercise the gift of showing mercy. Later we find Philip a successful evangelist (Acts 8:4-8, 26-40). Probably the faithful use of his earlier gifts of wisdom and showing mercy led to the discovery of his gift of evangelism. Faithfulness in one area may lead to a wider ministry.

Possession of a gift mandates its employment. We are to stir up our dormant gifts.

Delight

When a person discovers his gift and a place of ministry for it, he may well exclaim, "I've found it! This is it!" This has been called the "Eureka" principle (*The Greening of the Church*, F. B. Edge, Word Books, Waco, Texas).

When a member of Christ's body is rightly related to the Head, that member should enjoy ministering his gift. Conversely, endurance instead of enjoyment, frustration instead of fulfillment, suggests your task is not aligned with your gifts.

And this delight continues. Later he will enthusiastically affirm, "This is what I'd rather be doing for the Lord than anything else in the world. I so enjoy it! This is my thing. This turns me on!" He will readily talk about his ministry and wish to improve it. He will eagerly orate on its possibilities and bubble over it.

This "delight" criterion in discovering one's gifts seems equivalent to the "peace of God" principle in ascertaining God's will. A person who has diligently sought the will of God, then moved out in obedient faith, may find added corroboration in the inner peace of God. "Let the peace of God rule in your hearts" (be the umpire to render a verdict that you are doing God's will—Col. 3:15). Likewise the inner joy a person experiences in exercising a gift may indicate that this is indeed that person's gift.

The delight a person finds in ministering his gift is subconsciously communicated to the recipients of his ministry. Because he is turned on, he will turn others on. The overflow of delight reinforces the exercise of a gift.

Sadly, on the other hand, those who exercise gifts out of mere oughtness come across negatively, and with a certain deadness. The adult Bible class teacher who emphasizes the excitement of living for Christ, but does so out of duty, will come through to the class in such a way as to negate the lesson he is trying to teach.

How wrong to assume that because we enjoy some particular service that this ministry cannot be God's will for us. Or to deduce that because something is distasteful, this must be God's plan for us. Wouldn't God more likely assign us gifts the employment of which bring pleasure, not misery? Like Jesus, in doing the Father's will we should find delight, not drudgery.

It's not surprising that the word for gift (*charisma*) is related to the word for joy (*chara*). Joy comes through employing our gifts in a divinely appointed ministry. Great self-satisfaction settles dove-like over our hearts when we know that we have come to the kingdom to use our gifts for such a time as this.

Discernment by Others

Because delight has subjective elements, a person should submit his "eureka" feeling to the scrutiny of loving and discerning brethren. The crowning confirmation that we do possess a gift is recognition of this gift by others.

As we are doing Christian service in obedience to the commands of Christ, others may see a gift in us long before we ourselves are aware of it. In fact, the joy and preoccupation of ministry may make us temporarily oblivious to the special abilities which the Spirit has given us. Thus the need of discernment by believers who surround us. A vital duty of Christians is to encourage fellow believers when they observe a gift.

Because the gift of encouragement was clearly evident, the apostles gave a disciple named Joseph a new name, "Son of Encouragement" or "Barnabas" (Acts 4:36).

One reason for the choice of seven particular men as deacons was their recognized ability of wisdom (Acts 6:3).

When Paul refused to take Mark on his second missionary journey, Barnabas was determined to help Mark develop his obvious gifts, even if it meant breaking with his old associate (Acts 15:36-39).

When Paul chose young Timothy to join his team, he first made sure that the youth was "well reported of by the brethren" in that vicinity, which recommendation doubtless included recognition of gifts as well as of moral conduct (Acts 16:1-3).

Church letters in apostolic days usually contained commendation of some traveling Christian's character and gifts, so that the itinerant brother would not only be accepted but also put to immediate service in the new fellowship without having to wait for his gifts to be identified. For example, when Apollos wished to travel into Achaia, the Ephesian brethren wrote the disciples of Achaia to welcome him, "Who, when he was come, helped them much" (Acts 18:27).

In his very early Christian years, Paul's gifts and mission to the Gentiles were affirmed by the pillars of the Jerusalem church (Gal. 2:9).

Deacons, before election to that office, are to be "first proved" which would involve discernment of their gifts by fellow members (1 Tim. 3:10).

Others frequently recognize that we don't possess a gift we think we have. A young man home from Bible school at Christmas asked if he could give a short talk in the evening service. His material and delivery proved pathetic. The next Christmas he again asked for the same privilege. Again he flopped. Before the third Yule season rolled around, the pastor wrote the school about the young man's progress. When the school replied that he had no evident gifts for preaching, nor had made any apparent improvement in all his years at school, the pastor refused to let him preach that third Christmas, informing him on his visit home that others failed to recognize any preaching gift in him.

"Whoso boasteth himself of a false gift is like clouds and wind without rain" (Prov. 25:14).

Frank discussion with fellow believers may help identify our gifts. In a small group a young man who had been teaching Sunday School a year spoke up, "I'm wondering if teaching is really my gift?"

A friend commented, "I'm sure you have the gift of government. You're so good at organizing people to work together." With a flash of insight he saw that his gift lay more in the direction of government than teaching.

Because self-estimate may be colored by deception, our character and abilitites are often best evaluated by others. One professor said, "It's so strange to meet someone who claims to have the gift of preaching when no one has the gift of listening." Schools and businesses, in judging applications of prospective students or employees, require references from those who have observed the applicant through the years, such as previous employer, pastor, friend, teacher, neighbor. Objective opinions help balance delusions of grandeur or self-disparaging groveling. The would-be seminary student is usually required to secure the endorsement of his home church. A license to preach is recognition by a local fellowship of the candidate's gifts for the ministry. Before missionary candidates are commissioned for overseas service, they must usually be accepted by a missionary board.

The laying on of hands at an ordination service carries no sacred unction, but rather signifies human acknowledgement of previous divine anointing. This symbolic gesture, rich and beautiful, says, "We confirm that God has laid His hand on you. We recognize your divine call. As fellow servants we join with you in unity. As you go, we go with you."

Incidentally, no command is given regarding the laying on of hands, nor is this practice mentioned as a prerequisite to the reception of a gift.

Sometimes earthly fellowships do not recognize gifted men at first. Campbell Morgan was rejected as a candidate for the ministry at age 25. His father wired him, "Rejected on earth, accepted in heaven." In the next 25 years, Dr. Morgan won world-wide recognition as pastor, author, college president, and Bible teacher.

Only after painstaking preparation and two rejections for ordination was John Newton, author of *Amazing Grace,* finally ordained just before his 40th birthday by the Church of England. More than one successful missionary has sailed to a foreign field on his own because he was rejected by a missionary society, only to find acceptance a few years later.

Conclusion

The well-known English pulpiteer, Charles H. Spurgeon, visiting an elderly lady in an almshouse, noticed on the wall a frame encasing a piece of paper with some writing on it, so asked about it. The lady replied that it reminded her of an aged invalid man she had nursed many years before, who, appreciative of her kind care, had written his name on it in his final days. So she had framed it. After much persuasion Spurgeon was able to borrow the paper. When he took it to the bank, they exclaimed, "We've been wondering to whom the old gentleman left his money." Hundreds of pounds were standing idle to his credit which now were transferred to her name. Living in poverty for years, she had actually been worth a great deal.

It's possible for believers to live many years unconscious of their wealth of spiritual gifts. No wonder so much Christian service remains undone. If sufficient qualified workers seem to be missing from the Lord's work, blame cannot be attributed to the Holy Spirit, but to those who neglect or resist Him. The body of every believer enshrines the Holy Spirit who longs to see us discover and develop the gifts He has placed within. How much hidden treasure resides in every church! Unused gifts squander the grace of God.

Some believers who used their gifts in bygone days have allowed these gifts to cool almost into ashes. To such comes the reminder of Paul, "Stir up the gift of God which is in thee" (2 Tim. 1:6). The verb *stir,* found only here in the New Testament, means to rekindle slumbering ashes into a flame. Remember, once God gives a gift, He does not take it back. "The gifts . . . of God are without repentance" (Rom. 11:29).

The Book of Revelation graphically pictures Christ *outside the door of a church* (3:20). Perhaps He is standing at your heart's door saying, "I have given you gifts." Perhaps He is knocking, "I plead with you to discover them." And calling, "I desire you to use them for My glory in the service of others."